For Prodigals & Other Sinners

For Prodigals & Other Sinners

Landrum P. Leavell

BROADMAN PRESS
Nashville, Tennessee

Library of Congress Catalog Card Number: 72-90041

Printed in the United States of America

To my beloved wife, JoAnn Paris Leavell,
from whom I have learned the incomparable truth that
"It is not good for man to be alone."

For Prodigals & Other Sinners

CONTENTS

1

THE PRODIGAL SON

Luke 15:11-24

By any standard of measurement, chapter fifteen of the Gospel of Luke is one of the greatest chapters in all of literature, either secular or sacred. It has been the subject and the source for untold thousands of sermons from the time it was recorded, and yet this fifteenth chapter of Luke has often been abused and misinterpreted and we've been guilty of isolating it from the larger gospel truths.

Approached from any angle, we find revealed herein the heart of the gospel of Jesus Christ. This parable and the others that comprise chapter fifteen describe the inexpressible joy that comes to the heart of God through finding or recovering a lost sinner and restoring that one to the family relationship with himself.

The parable of our text is actually the story of two sons. I want it plainly understood that our text is only a portion of this parable, for we're considering one of these sons. Though it is the story of two sons, they both suffered a common malady. Both of these sons were guilty sinners. The one called the prodigal did what any individual must do if he is to come into the family relationship with God the Father. The other son, the one

11

whom we call the elder brother, remained unchanged in his disposition, his attitude, and his sinful self-righteousness. These two sons must be considered together, but for the purpose of this chapter we will point out only the life and testimony of the prodigal son.

I believe every human being can find his counterpart in this parable. You and I are identified either with the prodigal son, who in repentance and faith returned to his father, or we are like the elder brother, who in the hardness and arrogance of his own proud, sinful heart stayed outside the fellowship and love of his father. I see three things in this parable which I want to underscore. I see here lostness, light, and love. Let's look at

Lostness

first of all. The fact is the prodigal son's lost condition was not future, it was present. He was lost in the very moment he chose to get what was coming to him and leave home. You see, one does not die and go to hell in order to be lost. One is lost from the very instant he wilfully rejects Jesus Christ. In the moment one decides to go it alone, to do what he's going to do by himself, spurning the offer of God's love, direction, and companionship, in that moment one becomes a lost individual.

Just as eternal life begins in the instant of regeneration, so eternal lostness and condemnation begins in the moment, the instant, of wilful refusal to accept Jesus Christ. You don't have to go to hell in order to be lost. You can walk on the face of this earth, enjoying good health, in apparent prosperity, surrounded by friends, and be lost and condemned in the sight of almighty God. In the moment this young man said to his father, "I don't want any more of this," and turned his back to do his own thing, in that moment of decision he became lost.

I believe you would agree with me that this young man whom we call the prodigal son was 100 percent typical of the youth of our day and generation. He was a seeking, searching youth like those we know. It occurs to me that he had a dissatisfaction with life. He was gripped by a restlessness which led to a rejection of his parents' values. Everything his father had tried to teach him was thrown overboard. Every influence that had been brought to bear upon his life in the home of his parents he spurned and said, "I'm cutting out." He concluded the only avenue open to him was to protest against the establishment, which is exactly what he did when he left the home of his father. He left home to go to a distant city and join the ranks of other youthful protesters, to participate in their marches and do the things that they were doing in the big city.

I can imagine that he let his hair grow. I expect it was just a matter of time until he ceased to shave. You couldn't tell where his sideburns ended and his beard began. I can imagine that it was just a short time until his clothes were smelly and filthy, conforming to the clothes of all the other nonconformists, everyone looking exactly alike. But he thought he was doing his thing.

This was something he felt he had to do. He rejected his father, his family home, the childhood concepts he had been taught from his earliest recollection, and the standards of morality that had been shown him from childhood. All of this became passé and antiquated, and was thrown out when he received his inheritance and left the home of his father.

Sadly enough, this young man, like many youth in our day, thought this was freedom. Little did he realize that this was actually the worst kind of slavery at all. This was and is the very essence of slavery, the height and depth, the length and the breadth of it, for he had become a slave to himself. He bent his knee in obeisance to his own sinful whims and desires. He was looking out for number one, defining all of life in terms of "I want." Anything he wanted, he got. That, in reality, is the lowest and basest form of slavery. This young hippie originally thought of himself more highly than he ought to have, for he was living his life by the philosophy, "I'll do it my way." I expect you have heard the popular song in which this is stated: "And more, much more than this, I did it my way."

This young hippie we call the prodigal son had reached the point in life where he felt he didn't need his father's advice. After all, his father was over thirty years of age, and though he was a young man, he thought he had all the answers. He wanted to assert his own independence and that's precisely what he set about to do.

Let me hasten to state that there is nothing wrong with self-assurance, self-reliance, and self-confidence, for these are the attributes that have made America a great nation. These are the personality characteristics that have marked every great American patriot from the beginning of this land. There's nothing wrong with these in themselves, but when these characteristics lead to a rejection of God and an overthrow of authority, then these become sinful. This young man had a great deal of self-confidence, but like many young people, he thought he knew everything. He didn't want to listen to the advice of any older person; he wanted to do it his way.

This is the attitude of lost people, for lost men in our city will say quickly, "Look, I don't see anything so terribly wrong with me. Why is it that you've come to talk with me about my relationship to God? After all, I pay for everything I buy. I look after my family. I mind my own business. I vote in the election. I'm a good citizen. What's wrong with me?" Basically that lost man is saying, "Let me alone; I'm living a life that pleases me and that's all that matters." What a tragic way to live life, for that's the sort of life patterned after the demons in hell. Demons were perverting the life of a young man, and when they encountered Jesus Christ cried out, "Thou Jesus, Son of God, what have we to do with thee? Let us alone." The demons that occupy human beings today, many of whom live in higher priced homes, on the better streets in our cities, many of whom are in the top income bracket, cry out, "Let us alone, let us alone."

This was the attitude of the prodigal son. He didn't want his daddy looking over his shoulder telling him what to do. He didn't want advice from an older person. His attitude was "let me alone, let me live my life, let me stand on my own two feet." Dear friends, that is the heart of lostness. It is the lostness that marks the life of the prodigal son. It's still the characteristic of lost people in our city as well as up and down the land today. But thank God, this lost young man came one day to see the

Light

This young dropout from society whom we call the prodigal thought he was all right and out of sight. He thought he was where the action was but he was like the deluded person constantly seeking a pot of gold at the end of the rainbow. He was running after an elusive mirage. That for which he was looking could not be found in the place in which he was searching. It wasn't there. It was a mirage, yet when he thought he had it within his grasp it turned into ugliness and ashes.

I believe this young man saw the light when he summoned the courage for encounter. I like these bumper stickers which ask, "Have you the courage for encounter?" That's probably the biggest question you'll ever face in all your life, most especially if that encounter is one with the living, risen Christ. When he summoned the courage for encounter, it was then he came to himself.

Now for most people this is the first step in the home-
ward journey. Maybe this young man paused long
enough on his toboggan slide into hell to ask himself
some penetrating, all-important questions. Perhaps he
looked in the mirror long enough to ask, "Exactly what
are my values in life? What do I prize more highly than
anything else? What is the *summum bonum* of life for
me? What is it for which I would sell my soul?"

Have you ever faced up to those all-important, penetrating questions? Have you ever asked yourself,
"Where am I going in life? What are my goals? What
do I wish to achieve in my days on earth? To what am
I giving myself? Am I expending all of my energies in
things that will not last? Have I been deceived by a
diabolical plot of the devil to use up all my energies in
things that are not eternal?" Many a human being
ought to ask such questions of himself.

That may have been the moment when the light
came to this prodigal, or maybe it was the moment he
paused to look around and see that scurvy, crummy
crowd he was running with. Possibly he took one look
at his associates and cried, "What under heaven am I
doing with a crowd like this?" Could it be that it was
the moment he said to himself, "I'm my father's son and
I've got no business being with a sorry crowd of people
like this. Who are they? They're nothing! They're going
nowhere and they've come from nowhere. They have
no purpose in life whatever. They have no depth, no

seriousness of purpose; they are merely living for the present moment." They were probably the jet-set of the first century. They were being catapulted from one pot party to another, from one tavern to the next, and I suppose each one of them could talk from experience about his latest trip on LSD. That's the crowd he was running with. Who are they? They're nobodies— they're nothings. All of them added together will still equal zero.

That was the so-called "now" generation. They were the ones who were saying, "Let's live it up; let's try it all. There may not be a tomorrow and whatever avenue is open to us, let's walk that road. Let's find out what life is all about. We don't have to save anything for marriage; we don't have to deny ourselves any urge, all we have to do is live it up right now." It was in the midst of that kind of life the light finally broke through. The moment of truth came, the great discovery was made. It was at such a moment this dedicated young hippie suddenly reminded himself, "I am my father's son. I was not born to live with these hogs. Even the humblest, lowliest servant in the house of my father is better off than I am."

Maybe he had to sink as low as he could sink before the light could penetrate the blackness of his own ego and selfishness. Think of the come-down it must have been for this self-assured, articulate young intellectual, who thought he had all the answers, to suddenly realize he was on the bottom. He was flat on his back and there was no place where he might ever go to sink any deeper into sin and slime and stink than he had sunk. He was at the bottom. No Jewish lad could get lower than he, for he was having to earn what living he made feeding hogs. In the Jewish concept all pork was defiling and unclean. The text says that he would "feign have filled his belly with the husks" that he was feeding the hogs. Even the gristles in that hog slop would have been a palatable meal for him, he had sunk so low.

Then light came, in the form of his own identity. He suddenly realized who he was. He suddenly understood he was not made to live like that. This was not the highest life had to offer; in reality it was the lowest. You know, when that light comes it is the work of God's Holy Spirit, for that's what the Spirit does. He convicts us of who we are and who Christ is, and lets us know that back home there is a loving Father waiting to receive us with open arms. That brings us to the third point, which is

Love

We can scarcely understand this kind of love because we don't see much of it in evidence about us. Yet if we're going to understand the meaning of this parable, we've got to take it in light of verses 1 and 2 in this fifteenth chapter. In those verses we find that the scribes and the Pharisees have been critical of our Lord because he received sinners and ate with them. In other words, they were criticizing him for his associates. They were complaining, "What are you doing running around with people like that? Why aren't you associating with those of us that are good, religious people? Why do you have anything to do with a sinner and with a tax collector? Why do you spend time with harlots and people of the kind?"

If these critics had understood anything at all about God, if they had any comprehension whatever of the abject sorrow in the heart of God over the loss of one sinner, if they had had any conception of his indescribable, his unfathomable elation over the salvation of one hippie who turns around and comes home, they wouldn't have been critical! They'd have known what the love of God is all about. They would never have dared to raise a voice in criticism of Jesus running around with people whom the rest of the world despised. The reason Jesus did that sort of thing was because they were people who needed what only Jesus was offering them. The world had already cut them off, just like the world had already cut off this prodigal. They said, "He made his bed, now let him lie in it. He made his own choice, let him have it. If that's what he wants to do, if he wants to destroy himself, let him destroy himself."

All the neighbors and everyone who knew what the prodigal had done washed their hands of him, all but one. That was the Father. That boy's daddy couldn't turn him loose. He couldn't forget him, day in and day out, night after night. He spent restless hours rolling and tossing in the anguish of his soul, wondering where his boy was, wondering if his boy ever thought about home and if he'd ever see that boy again. What's Jesus trying to say in this parable? He's trying to say to you and me, when we've wandered into that far country of sin, that God is like the father who never gave up on his boy, who never locked the gate where his boy couldn't come back, but left it swinging wide day and night yearning, hoping, praying that one day the boy would come to his senses and return home.

Recall what happened in the story when the boy came home. This is what God is like. This is the way God will receive you as a prodigal. There was no recitation of his aberrations. There was no recital of the sins he had committed. There was no condemnation for his foolishness and lack of judgment. There was no denunciation for his crawling home, filthy dirty, and flat broke; not a word of condemnation for any of that. On the other hand there was a banquet. The father called all the servants and told them to pick the finest and best meal they had ever served in that house, and put it out there on the table. He told some other servants to go and get the best robe that was on the place, find some shoes for his boy's feet, and get the ring he had been saving and put that ring on the boy's finger. "This is my boy and he's home; he was lost but he has returned again."

Then the prodigal made another mistake. It was the opposite of the first one he made. His first mistake was when he thought of himself more highly than he ought to think, and when he got home he thought of himself less highly than he ought to have thought. He said to his father, "I'm no more worthy to be called thy son, just let me be like one of your servants." The thing he didn't understand was the love of the father and the willingness of the father to reinstate his status as his son and one of his heirs.

This kid who left home as a hippie thought that life and a living were the same things. His father gave him part of the living, the part that was coming to him, but money and things don't give life. That's where the young man came to his senses. You see, he found life where he originally had missed it. He found it in the house of the father whom he had rejected. That's the irony of life as it's being lived by prodigals all over the world. When they reject God and the Father's house, little do they realize that they're rejecting life, for the only source of life is in the Father's house, in the family relationship, when they pay obeisance to him and become obedient children in his home.

The only mistake the prodigal made when he came home was that common mistake of thinking of himself less highly than he ought to have thought. Lost people often say, "I'm not worthy, I'm not worthy." Dear friend, that's not the point. No one of us is worthy, but "God commended his love toward us in that while we were yet sinners, Christ died for us." That's the point of it all. We don't have to be anything. God is the One who is something, and God offers us his love and a place in his home, not as a hired servant or a slave, but as his own child. Maybe the lost person says, "I can't hold out. How do I know, if I give my heart to Jesus and trust him, that I'll be able ten years from now to follow Christ in devotion and dedication? How do I know I can live up to it?" Dear friend, don't question God's love and power, just do your part. You just come home, God will do the rest. He'll not chastise you, he'll not condemn you, he'll not kick you away from the door, but he'll throw open the door and with loving arms receive you and pardon you and give you status in his home as his child.

Wherever you may have wandered, however far you may have gotten from the Father's house, he's ready right now to take you back. He'll receive you. He'll give you a place in his house, a place of service, a place of challenge and opportunity. Will you accept his offer? If you will, the opportunity is yours right now. Take your stand publicly on Christ's side, following him in sincerity for salvation or for service.

2

THE OTHER SINNER

Luke 15:25–32

If I were to give you a pencil and a piece of paper and ask you to list the cardinal sins in order, what would your list reveal? I expect most of us would begin by listing murder as the worst sin of all. This is a heinous crime, both against mankind and God. In descending order we would list other sins according to our own particular world view. Possibly the next worst sin, in the minds of some, would be adultery. Then would come stealing and next we'd possibly put lying. Maybe on another line we'd put the sin of cheating and a little farther down the list the sin of drunkenness. On we'd go, making out the list according to our own reasoning.

It was exactly at this point that Jesus upset the thinking of the scribes and Pharisees. You see, they had sin well categorized. Their estimate of sin was that of which the other man was guilty, and they overlooked that which they themselves had committed. This is largely true of us today. I doubt that we know many murderers. We're pharisaical to claim murder is the worst sin of all just because it's a sin we haven't committed! The truth is we ordinarily refer to our personal sins as "little sins." We think of them in an entirely different light. Yet a burden of the ministry of Jesus Christ was to teach that the sins of the spirit are just as heinous in the sight of God as the sins of the flesh.

I believe that's the reason our Lord gave us this parable. It's a contrast. In the parable we discover two sons whose sins are at different ends of the spectrum. One is guilty of the sins of the flesh. Everyone knew his sin, for he had wasted his inheritance among the harlots with wine, women, and song as the consuming passion of his life. No one could help but know his sins. His were obvious, but Jesus gave us the story of two sons and both of them are sinners. The older brother, though not guilty of the sins of the flesh, is guilty of the sins of the spirit and Jesus taught that these were as bad in God's sight as the sins of the flesh. May God help us to learn this lesson and see ourselves in the same light in which God sees us.

The Pharisees, though they were meticulously moral, were guilty in the sight of God because of their sins of the spirit. On one occasion our Lord said that publicans and harlots would get into the kingdom of God ahead of the scribes and Pharisees. When we understand that statement it becomes frightening. It scares us because we must confess that there is no one of us who is living as clean a life as those Pharisees and scribes. When Jesus said the worst sinners of all, in the sight of society, would get into the Kingdom ahead of these religious people, we'd better delve more deeply into the meaning of that and discover what Jesus was teaching.

It's my conviction that he was teaching that the sins of the flesh and the sins of the spirit are equally reprehensible in the sight of God. Now just because we don't happen to be guilty of one category of sin does not give us any advantage in God's sight over those who are guilty of that sin, but who are innocent of the sins we've committed. The point seems to be that all of us are sinners, and when we choose our particular brand of sin we don't necessarily gain favor with God. When our sins are hidden, sins of the spirit, we nevertheless stand condemned.

I recall the story of a young man who fell in love with a New England preacher's daughter. He went to the preacher to ask for his daughter's hand in marriage. To his utter surprise he was refused. He asked the father in amazement, "Why can't I marry your daughter?" The answer came, "If I gave you permission to marry her you couldn't live with her." In even greater amazement he asked, "Why, she's a Christian isn't she?" The answer was, "Yes, son, but when you've lived as long as I have, you'll discover that there are some people God can live with that nobody else can."

Do you remember the story of the three bears: the mama bear, the papa bear, and baby bear? Papa bear and baby bear had been out in the woods playing all morning and came in at noon. Rushing into the dining room, they picked up their soup bowls, turned them upside down and the papa bear cried, "Somebody drank my soup." Baby bear said: "Somebody drank my soup." Mama Bear came in and said, "Shut up your yakkity yak, I haven't even poured the soup!"

Then there is the one about the old grouch who had been married to this longsuffering, dear, sweet lady for forty years, during which time he had never complimented her. She'd never done anything right, but being of the disposition that she was, she kept on trying. One morning she got up a long time before the usual breakfast hour, fixed her face, dressed completely, had her hair all combed, and came in where the old grouch was reading the paper. She asked, "Darling, how would you like your eggs?" He looked over the paper and snarled, "I want one fried and one scrambled." She smiled sweetly and disappeared into the kitchen. After a time she completed her preparations and presented to him a plate of eggs beautifully cooked, little pieces of parsley adorning the plate, and everything total perfection. She stepped back, waiting for him to say a kind word. About that time the tirade began! He "lit in" and was vehement in his denunciation of everything. She burst into tears and cried, "What in the world is the matter now?" With a snarl he answered, "You fried the wrong egg!"

It may be you know someone like that. But the question I'm asking is, "Are you like that?" That gets a little closer to home, doesn't it? I'm not trying to suggest that the prodigal son was innocent, but I am saying that between the prodigal son and the older brother, the sin of the older brother is far more prevalent today. You can probably name the prodigals known to you on the fingers of one hand, but you cannot begin to name the elder brothers you know who are guilty of a hellish disposition. Look with me at these

Sins

of the spirit. Nothing, absolutely nothing so quickly negates your Christian testimony as a foul, festering spirit. Nothing makes people question the validity of your experience with Christ more quickly than this ugly disposition, which constantly causes antagonism and bitterness.

Do I need to remind you that it is entirely possible that the older brother is the reason that the prodigal son left home? That is a strong possibility. I don't know how you feel, but there are some things I simply will not live with. I don't intend to live in a home that is a little civil war. I'm not made that way. In fact, I told a certain person before we were married that I would not fight with her to live with her, and if she was looking for a fight, she'd better keep looking because I did not intend to live in that kind of atmosphere!

Maybe the prodigal son was fed up with living in the midst of bitterness and criticism. Possibly he reached the breaking point and said, "I'm through! I won't live in this another day." He went to his daddy and said, "Whatever I've got coming to me, give it here, I'm leaving." It could well be that the older brother was the reason he left home.

I wonder how many marriages have gone on the

rocks because of a foul disposition? A critical spirit that accompanies a foul disposition proves what's on the inside. I want to tell you, there's no way Jesus Christ can live in you without making a difference in your disposition. If Jesus lives in you, your spirit will be Christlike. Your disposition will reflect the difference. There'll be a noted change in your entire outlook when Christ is Lord of your life.

There's a certain psychology to be found in criticism. Ordinarily it's an attempt to cover up one's own sin. When you spend your time trying to tear down someone else, the psychology is you're trying to keep someone from criticizing you. You believe that if someone can be turned in the direction of another party, then he won't be looking closely at your life. Every time you point an accusing index finger in another direction, you've got three fingers pointing right back at yourself!

The older brother possessed a critical spirit. He wasn't happy at all when the younger brother returned home. I've known persons to say, "I just say what I think. I can't help it, I'm just frank about how I feel." Listen, you're not frank, you're mean! There's no way you can cover up your kind of disposition behind the guise of frankness. It's hellishness and it is not like Jesus! Now if you claim to be a Christian, you're claiming to be like Jesus. If you're not like Jesus, don't blame him for your meanness. Don't say you're being like Jesus when you're acting like the devil.

I once knew a lady who blamed frankness for her evil disposition. She was one of those who fit a description I heard given by Dr. Lee. He described a lady who had a tongue long enough to stand in the living room and lick grease out of the skillet in the kitchen! This certain lady had hurt more feelings and had run rough shod over more human beings than any person I've ever known. She was small of stature, she was flippant, and she'd shrug her shoulders after a particularly deep cut, and smirk, "I'm sorry, but I'm just frank about how I feel." It wasn't frankness at all, it was an unregenerate disposition. Jesus had nothing to do with that sort of spirit.

A foul disposition is one of the sins of the spirit. Envy is another. Envy works in an unusual way, for it is actually a paradox. It makes us unhappy over the success of someone else, and makes us happy over someone's downfall. Do you know what I mean? You've felt that, haven't you? There isn't an honest person but who would have to admit he has felt envy. You've looked at what someone else has, and wished they did not have it. You've seen someone else topple and you've been secretly glad they've gone under. Envy usually makes us happy when someone else fails.

When a member of the church is known to be guilty of gross sin, isn't that the time that he needs us the most? Rather than being critical and little and mean toward such a person, rather than trying to push away and have nothing to with such a one, isn't that the one who most needs the spirit of Jesus in us, reaching out in love and compassion and forgiveness?

The sins of the disposition are many. Self satisfaction is another. The older brother was guilty of self-satisfaction. The text said so. He said to the father, "Lo, these many years I've served thee. I never did take any money, run out and spend it all, and come home filthy dirty, flat broke, and stinking. I didn't ever do anything like that." In other words, look at me! If this kid brother was just doing as well as I'm doing, everything would be fine. We all have that tendency, don't we? We are all prone to look at other folks and conclude if they just do as well as we're doing, if they'd serve the Lord the way we're serving, everything would be fine.

Americans, in the main, have been afflicted by this same philosophy. Most of us believe that if the rest of the world would cut out it's meanness, we'd have a pretty good place to live. Yet we're the only nation on the face of the earth that ever dropped an atomic bomb on another nation! No, we can't locate all of the problems with other people, yet self-satisfaction creeps in so quickly and destroys us so completely.

When the older brother came in from the fields that night, after working all day, he heard the sounds of joy at the big house. He couldn't stand it. He didn't even want to find out what was going on, so he stood outside pouting. I can understand a child pouting. We've got four at our house, and I've seen them all go through that. We've nearly got the last one through that stage.

I can understand a six year old having a fat lip, puffed out, refusing to have anything to do with anybody as an evidence of displeasure, but I can't get ready for it in a grown person. When we grow up physically, we ought to grow up emotionally. This older brother had never grown up. He was just plain mad that his younger brother, who had been given up for dead, was now found alive. He was not willing to accept it. His daddy had to come out where he was, pat him on the back and plead, "Come on now big brother, don't be mad. Everything's going to be all right. Come on in and tell your brother that you're glad he's back home. Please come in." Can you imagine?

Is it possible that a born-again believer in Christ would adopt such an unspeakably evil attitude? Is it possible that a member of a Sunday School class would say, "Well I had my feelings hurt, and I'm not going back." Yes, unfortunately it's possible. I talked with such a one just recently. How sad it is to see this. It's a clear evidence of sin. Not the kind of sin of which the prodigal was guilty, but the brand of sin of which the elder brother was guilty, and neither of these was exonerated in the parable Jesus told.

If you were going to take one of these brothers on a ten-day deer and elk-hunting trip to Colorado, which one would you want to go along with you, the prodigal son or the older brother? No one in his right mind would want to go anywhere with that older brother. He'd be thin lipped and churlish, making snide, catty remarks, He'd always do his part, but he'd never do one iota more. He'd never lend a helping hand to anyone else, and he'd always compare what he did with what you've done and make you show up in a bad light. The younger brother, though slightly immature, would be generous, jovial, happy, maybe a little unstable, but probably good company. Now I'm not saying that the prodigal was innocent. He wasn't. He was a sinner, but the point is, so was the older brother. Where we might have one prodigal son, we'd have dozens of older brothers in our midst. We've looked at these sins, now let's talk about their

Solution

I assume every sincere Christian wants a better disposition. We want to be more like Jesus Christ. I think it's high time that we took time out to tune up, and work toward a better disposition. It could be you'll be surprised when you get to heaven to find some of the folks who made it. But it also may be a surprise to some folks that you made it!

Have you ever wanted to write an anonymous letter? If you have, then you're the kind of person that fits this category, because you have the kind of disposition that makes a lot of people want to write you one!

We're busy. Most of us think on occasion we're the busiest person in the world. I've never found a person so busy that he didn't have enough time to tell someone else how busy he was. Let's take a busy moment and try to determine some steps that will lead us away from the sins of the spirit.

I would say the first step to a better disposition is honesty. By that I mean we must accept our limitations. We must recognize that God did not give us every talent we see in other human beings. At some point in life we have to face up to the fact that we cannot do all things well. Very few will be All-Americans in any sport. That's not important. The important thing is that you take what you have and use it.

I remember about twenty years ago when I made a great step forward in personality development. It was the day that I accepted the fact that I was not Billy Graham. I stopped trying to be like him. I decided if God had wanted me to be Billy Graham, that's who I would have been. He didn't want me to be Billy, he wanted me to be Landrum Leavell. I've lived long enough and grown enough in personality development to the point that I feel a little sorry for Billy now! He doesn't have the privileges and joys that God affords me, and I'm sorry for anybody that doesn't know the joy I know. Billy preaches to tens of thousands, but he never has the privilege that I had tonight of baptizing some people. He doesn't have the joy that I have of uniting a couple in marriage. He doesn't know the heaviness of heart a pastor experiences who stands with a beloved family in deep grief, and who walks with them beside the open grave. He knows little of this sort of thing.

The point is, God called him to do what he does and

he called me to do what I do. I'm not Billy Graham, nor is he Landrum Leavell. I can't sing like Lee Castro, but I'm going to get it on him one day! When we get to heaven, I'm going to take about a year and say, "Lee, you sit down and listen to me for awhile," and I'm going to sing to him.

You heard the story about the tenor who said his idea of heaven was to have a choir composed of twenty-thousand sopranos, thirty-thousand altos, ten thousand-basses and he was the only tenor!

Accept what God has given you. Accept it for what it is, and utilize it to the fullest. Don't try to be someone else. There's no reason for a Christian to have an inferiority complex. To whom should you ever feel inferior? Not a single person on the face of the earth. God made you, God loves you, God saved you, and he has a plan for your life. Find it and do it, and don't look in fear to anyone. Look every man straight in the eye and walk with your head erect, possessed by the assurance that you know him, whom to know aright means life everlasting. Be honest.

A second step is to exercise a spirit of charity toward other persons. This will do so much to eliminate a foul disposition. If you're constantly holding up the yardstick of perfection for other people, hold up that same yardstick for yourself. If you're willing to diminish the requirements personally, then diminish your requirements for others. Don't expect them to be perfect either. Come to the realization of the fact that God made us and endowed us with all of our capacities, yet we are still imperfect. Pause once in a while to laugh at your own mistakes. See yourself in the ridiculousness of the pompous attitude you sometimes show, and learn to laugh at yourself. When you do, you'll take a long step toward a more Christlike disposition.

The final step is probably the most important of all: develop the mind of Christ in you. How can you do this? You can saturate your mind with the teachings and truths of the Word of God. It's no problem to know God's will, for God's will is clearly outlined in the pages of the Book. It's there, so you don't have to say, "I don't know what God wants me to do." I know what his Word said. He wants you to be saved; he wants you to be a witness for him; he wants you to know the joys of life; he wants you to possess his peace beyond all understanding. All of this is God's will. He wants you to be faithful. Yes, you can know the mind of Christ for you through the study of his Word.

Let me give you a prescription. I think this will probably do as much to sweeten your disposition and make you more like Jesus as anything I know. Read the thirteenth chapter of 1 Corinthians frequently, and when the truth of that beautiful love chapter sinks into your mind and heart, one day you'll come to the realization that it is nothing but a portrait of Jesus, painted with a consummate artistry and skill of the apostle Paul. He is the One we are to be like. That's how we are to act, that's the kind of lives we're to live.

"Love suffereth long and is kind, love vaunteth not itself, is not puffed up, does not behave itself unseemly, seeketh not her own, is not provoked, thinketh no evil." All of these are but characteristics of Jesus, and then you come to that great resounding climax of it all. Here it is: "Love never faileth." Did you hear it? "Love never faileth." Love isn't a stop-and-go proposition. Love isn't here today and gone tomorrow. Love's not something you fall into and fall out of. Love never faileth. Just as the love of God for you and me is constant in spite of our imperfections, weaknesses, and sins, so our love for those about us ought to be constant.

Are you like that older brother? You don't have to be, you know. You can have the kind of disposition that will enable those around you to see Jesus living in you!

3

THE SHEPHERD'S PSALM

Psalm 23

By universal agreement, this is the pearl of the Psalms. It has been likened to a nightingale singing in an hour of loneliness and need. It has spoken to the hearts of Christians, both in times of joy and sorrow, from the day in which David wrote it to this good hour.

A little girl was asked one day in her Sunday School class, "What is your favorite passage of Scripture?" She replied quickly, "The Lord is my Shepherd, that's all I want." With that childish error she expressed the centrality of the Christian faith. "The Lord is my Shepherd, that's all I want."

This Psalm is divided naturally into three divisions. In our chapter and verse divisions of the Bible there are only six verses in it and each section contains two verses. The first two verses describe the

SHEPHERD and the SHEEP

Who among us has not committed this wonderful Psalm to memory? When we read it in the original language we learn some things about it that are meaningful to us today. Early Hebrew was written with consonants only. Of all the languages I've ever studied, Hebrew is the most difficult. It was required in graduate work that we have five languages, two of which were Greek and Hebrew. Of all the languages I've studied, Hebrew is by far the most laborious and difficult.

Can you imagine trying to read a language that had no vowels? That's the way early Hebrew was written. The vowels were added centuries after the language was committed to writing in the form of little jots and tittles written under the consonants. This is still true today. One's eye must catch the consonants above and the vowel beneath as he reads. Another interesting thing about Hebrew is that the language is printed in books beginning at the back and going to the front. They begin reading at the righthand side of the page and move to the left. Everything about it is foreign to languages we know and which we have studied.

In early Hebrew there were four consonants assigned to the name God. These are the four that appear here in Psalm 23. Our translation reads "the Lord." These four consonants are the ones translated that way. If we transliterated them into the English language they would be JHWH. Can you pronounce that? No, and that's precisely the way the Hebrews wanted it. They didn't intend for God's name to be pronounced by the lips of sinful human beings.

Scholars through the years have called these four consonants the tetra-grammaton. They're translated variously in different translations of the Old Testament. In some places they appear "the Lord," in some places "Jehovah," and scholars call these four "Jahveh." They refer to the God of transcendence, the God of might, the God of glory, the God of creative activity who in his omnipotence spoke and brought the world into being.

In early Hebrew times names were descriptive of character. This carried over even into the New Testament. You will recall that the name "Abraham" meant the father of mercy. The name Abram, which preceded it, meant the father of many. The word "Isaac" means laughter. It was given to the son born after the angel of God announced to Abraham and Sarah that they would be the parents of a child after they had reached ninety years of age. Sarah laughed at the angel who made the announcement, so the son's name was Isaac recalling that experience.

In New Testament times our Lord gave Simon a new name. The name was descriptive of the character that he would have under God's transforming grace and power. It was so in the days in which David wrote the Psalms. The One to whom he referred was One of moral purity and righteousness, One of all power. Can you understand now what David wrote here? The One who brought the world into being, the God from whom nothing is hidden, the One who even has the hairs of our heads numbered, the One who is aware of a sparrow falling to the earth in death, that One has assumed the position of Shepherd toward me! What a tremendous statement. The Lord, the God of Hosts, is my Shepherd.

But the emphatic word in this opening phrase is the little monosyllable, my. Grasp the depth of meaning here. This One, who made the world and all that's in it, is *my* Shepherd. That monosyllable makes all the difference in the world. In fact there's no salvation until you say, "The Lord is my Shepherd." If you really do know him, then you can join David in saying he is mine and I am his.

I heard of a Negro preacher who was preaching on the baptism of Jesus. In a beautifully descriptive phrase he referred to that scene where Christ, God's Son, stood in the waters of the Jordan River to be baptized of John. The Spirit of God descended in the form of a dove to light on the shoulder of Jesus. Then he said, "God the Father looked down from the parapets of heaven upon that beautiful scene and saw it was good, and God said, "That's my boy and I'm proud of him." That's not exactly what the King James translation says, but I believe he caught the spirit of it. My boy, I'm proud of him. The monosyllable makes all the difference in the world.

When one can say the opening phrase with David, he can also say the second, "I shall not want." This basically means, "I shall want for nothing." Today we've reached a point of utter confusion when it comes to a differentiation between our needs and our wants. We say we need something when the truth is we merely want it. There are only seven or eight basic needs humans have. These are things required for life to continue. We need food, clothing, air to breathe or oxygen, shelter from the cold, water. Beyond that everything becomes a want to a greater or lesser degree. In no place does God promise to supply our wants! Some of us have concluded if we're Christians God is going to take care of all our wants, and we ought to possess everything the material world has to offer. Nothing could be farther from the truth. The apostle Paul wrote, "My God shall supply all your needs according to his riches in glory through Jesus Christ." We need sunshine, we need rain, we need air to breathe, we need basic essentials of food and clothing and God has gloriously supplied them. That's all he promised to do. David, content with the fact that the Lord was his Shepherd wrote, "I shall not want." I shall want for nothing.

Madison Avenue has done an excellent job in whetting the wants of human beings. All of us have succumbed to the advertising and most of us possess "want lists," things that we want to buy. Just as soon as we are able to pay down on them, we are going to possess them. This is not what God promised us. This is materialistic and in many ways selfish, yet God has guaranteed the supply of our need.

David said concerning his Shepherd who supplied his needs, "He maketh me to lie down in green pastures." Sometimes God has to do this. You see, a thoughtful Shepherd was constantly in search of new pastures for his sheep. Those he found would be possessed of lush, green, verdant grass—a beautiful pasture! That's the kind the Shepherd wanted for his sheep. David said that even when it's necessary for my Shepherd to make me lie down, I find it's in a beautiful spot. It's not only healthy, but relaxing and invigorating.

Once in a while we come to occasions when God in his wisdom has to say, "It is enough; stop right where you are!" Sometimes it is in the form of a hospital experience; sometimes it is a doctor's order for us to desist from all activity, sometimes it's in the stark sorrow of the death of a loved one. Then we're pulled up short and see the error of our ways and the selfishness of our existence. We come at these moments to evaluate the meaningless experiences through which we are going and the ceaseless round of activity in which we are involved. We discover how utterly absurd it is. When he makes us lie down, it is in a green pasture and if we open our eyes and look around, we will see the blessings of God even in the midst of seeming adversity.

Verses 3 and 4 describe

The Guide and the Traveler

David wrote, "He leadeth me beside still waters." Being familiar with sheep, he knew a sheep wouldn't drink from noisy, running water. They'll only drink from a placid pond. What a message for our souls. Sometimes the way to get closer to God is not by accepting new and greater responsibilities, not trying to serve in more capacities; sometimes the way to get close to God is through being still to know that he is God. I believe David has it correctly here: "He leadeth me." I believe he is right because it is not our natural tendency to go to the still waters. It's our tendency to go faster and do more. In our age it is easier to turn on the television than it is to open the Bible. It's not hard to understand, for it's our nature to pick up the newspaper more readily than to fall to our knees in prayer. The fact is, when we go to the still waters he has to lead us to that point.

"He restoreth my soul." Keep in mind that your soul is your total life. You can't separate your soul from your physical body. If you do, death is the result. We need to underscore the truth that when we have tired bodies we are not in shape for a spiritual blessing.

On occasion friends have kidded me over the fact that some people sleep through my sermons. I personally can't understand how anyone could sleep through one of these pearls of wisdom, these gems of exposition, but on occasion it happens. I don't feel badly about it and will not feel intimidated by it unless you give me the privilege of setting their Saturday schedule. If you let me tell you what to do on Saturday, then I believe you'd stay awake on Sunday. You stay out half the night, go to bed late, wake up mad on Sunday morning, wishing that you could turn over and go back to sleep, but that internal compulsion gets you up to go to church. When you get there, you're mad, fussing at the family, snapping and growling like cats and dogs, and finally reach Sunday School. Maybe you listen a little as you're personally involved, but then you come into the auditorium; air-conditioned in the summer, heated in the winter, a beautiful auditorium with cushioned seats, and what happens? Now you don't have to be a prophet to know what happens.

If Jesus himself were standing there preaching, your tired body would still cry out for sleep and chances are good you'd drop off into the arms of Morpheus. Is that because the preacher didn't make adequate preparation? No! As a preacher, I'll accept the blame for preaching some very poor sermons. That's far too often, but I can't accept the blame for people with tired bodies sleeping through a worship service. "He restoreth my soul." If you want a spiritual blessing, don't be unmindful of your physical needs. You need adequate sleep, you need a proper diet, you need an ample amount of exercise, and without these it's not unusual for you to have "tired blood" and drop off to sleep whenever you sit still.

"He leadeth me in the paths of righteousness for his name's sake." You know, these paths are wagon ruts of righteousness. It's interesting that this is where God leads us. I believe it's not so much a matter of picking and choosing what we're going to do as it's a matter of letting him lead. When he leads, he'll always lead in paths of righteousness.

Does God lead you to rob him of his tithe? No, God doesn't do that. When God leads, he leads in right paths. He leads you to the fulfilment of his will. God will never lead you to break his law. When you break God's law, be honest enough to say it is selfishness and the promptings of Satan that have made you do that. Use Flip Wilson's philosophy: "The devil made me do it." That's more accurate. God does not lead anyone to break his law.

We do all this "for his Name's sake." Why do you go to church? I'm reminding all of us that if we attend church for any other reason or for any other motive than for his name's sake, we're on the wrong track. If we serve for his name's sake, we're on the right track. If we serve for his name's sake, we'll never quit. If we give our money for his name's sake, we'll never stop. We're not giving to be seen of men, or to build a reputation for ourselves, but for his name's sake. That's the motive which prompts a Christian.

When he leads us in paths of righteousness, he leads us there for his name's sake. God's name is descriptive of his character, his reputation, his standing in the minds of men, and that's the image we're trying to enhance. Therefore, when we walk in paths of righteousness, we do it for the honor and glory of Jesus Christ.

"Yea, though I walk through the valley of the shadow of death, I will fear no evil: for thou art with me; thy rod and thy staff they comfort me." It was necessary in David's day to move the sheep frequently. Good pastures ran out quickly in that dry, arid country. David described an experience well known to his peers. One would often lead his sheep through dark, narrow valleys and gorges, where not only bandits lurked to prey upon innocent travelers but also wild beasts would descend upon defenseless animals. Ordinarily, going through the valley of the shadow of death, one would quicken his pace.

Do you ever remember having run home at night when dark caught you away? Possibly you were visiting the home of a friend. Maybe in the old days, out in the country, it was down the road a quarter of a mile. You weren't aware of it, but darkness had fallen. When you came out, realized it was time to go home and saw it was dark, your heart leaped up in your throat. When you started down that road, looking in both directions with furtive glances, you broke into a run. That's natural, isn't it? It was natural in David's day. He said for those who know the Lord as a personal Shepherd, even in the valley of the shadow, even with death lurking all around, one can walk with an unhurried pace, looking neither to the right nor to the left, simply looking up.

The rod and the staff are useful instruments. "Rod" is the same word found in Proverbs where we read, "Spare the rod and spoil the child.'" It was a short, heavy club the shepherd used for punishment. Sometimes a sheep would lose it's head, begin bleating wildly, and run pell-mell with all the other sheep following. The shepherd had to be ready to turn such a sheep back to guard the safety of the others.

The staff was the long crooked instrument the shepherd would use to reach down, snare a sheep that had slipped over a precipice, and pull him back to safety.

David said the Lord has a rod and staff, and it's a comfort to know that God not only has them, but uses them.

In the last two verses we find a description of

The Host and the Guests

"Thou preparest a table before me in the presence of mine enemies." If you're one of those who has said, "If I have an enemy in the world, I don't know it," don't ever say that again! You're admitting you're not like Jesus. If a man is like Jesus, he's going to have some enemies. Make certain the enemies you have are those at enmity with you because of your Christian convictions and the stand you've taken for Jesus Christ. David said even with the enemies all around, God prepared him a banquet feast where he sits at the table and eats. The enemies are there, maybe barking, maybe nipping at his heels, but impotent to molest him! A table is prepared in the presence of one's enemies.

"Thou anointest my head with oil." Hebrew homes kept a vial of oil that was used to anoint the head of a loved one at the time of homecoming. Maybe one had been on a long journey. In those days when communications were poor, they wouldn't know from week to week whether or not the absent loved one was still alive. In rejoicing, in gratitude when he would return home, the vial of oil would be brought out and one's head would be anointed. David said this is the way God treats those who come home. He has a vial of oil and will anoint your head when you come to him.

"My cup runneth over." This signifies abundance in

a land where starvation was common. It's little wonder that David said not merely a full cup, but one that's overflowing and running into the saucer. What a beautiful picture for people who knew what it was to have water shortages, famines, and food shortages, and who knew what it was to go to bed hungry and thirsty at night.

Then David exclaimed, "Surely goodness and mercy shall follow me all the days of my life: and I will dwell in the house of the Lord for ever." This word surely could be translated "only." Think of it like that. "Only goodness and mercy shall follow me all the days of my life: and I will dwell in the house of the Lord for ever." That means when moving day comes and we shed this old earthly tabernacle, we don't even leave the Lord's house, we just move upstairs to continue our eternal existence.

Eternal life has quality, but even more it has quantity. It is forever, and for those who can say, "The Lord is my Shepherd," it means dwelling with our Shepherd in his sheepfold forever and forevermore.

Can you sense the aura of victory that surrounds this beautiful Psalm? That victory can be yours if you're willing to submit your will to his will and say in sincerity, "The Lord is my Shepherd."

The songwriter must have been thinking of this Psalm when he penned these words:

Saviour, like a shepherd lead us,
Much we need thy tender care;
In Thy pleasant pastures feed us,
For our use Thy folds prepare:
Blessed Jesus, blessed Jesus,
Thou hast bought us, Thine we are.
Blessed Jesus, blessed Jesus,
Thou hast bought us, Thine we are.

4

GOD'S CURE FOR DELINQUENCY

Deuteronomy 6:4–9

Every year along in the spring we have an observance in the Southern Baptist Convention called Christian Home Week. This usually comes about the time we observe Mother's Day. Perhaps you, like I, have thought basically that this is rather trite. Why, under heaven, would we have to observe Christian Home Week with the families represented in the churches? Isn't this a little absurd? When we go beyond the superficial, we find it is not absurd or trite, but that it is one of the most needed emphases we give in our day and time.

Statistics reveal the failure of the home today. The crime rate is going up at a rapidly mounting pace, and the area of crime growing the most rapidly is crime being committed by teen-agers or juveniles. I personally believe that this is a pointed indictment against the homes of America; that we're training a bunch of teen-aged hoods and thugs, and turning them loose upon society. This is a positive indication of the breakdown of the home in the twentieth century. I don't have all the answers to be given to this problem, but I know in my own heart that the only way that we're going to shut

down this tidal wave of delinquency and stem this sta-
tistical flood is for American homes to come back to
those foundations upon which American homes previ-
ously were built. When our homes are like the homes
of our fathers and our grandfathers, and our grandfathers' fathers, then American children will be what our
forebears were. To me it's just that simple. If our homes
are to be what God would have them be, they've got
to be places of

Importance

Our text shows the relationship of the parent to the
importance of leadership. It clearly commands parents
to teach their children the things of the Lord. One of
the reasons for the astronomical divorce rate in our day
is our children have not been properly taught the cor-
rect concept of marriage. We must remember that the
home is the basic unit of society next to the individual.
Other than the individual, the home is the irreducible
minimum. Recall, if you will, that God said in the very
beginning, "It is not good for the man to be alone;
therefore, I will make for him an help meet." It was in
the divine economy that God created woman for man
and man for woman.

It is also interesting to note that God established the
home before he established his church. God could have
gone into the church business at any moment, but he
chose first to found the home. In the New Testament
Jesus Christ enlarges upon this same concept for he
said, "For this cause shall a man leave his father,

mother, sisters and brothers, and cleave only unto his wife." Therefore, the home is of importance.

Jesus said that in the sight of God when one man and one woman are joined together in the bonds of marriage, they become as one flesh in God's eyes. You can not sever "one flesh." You cannot divide a human being in half and expect him to live. When we get the proper concept of marriage and know the importance of the home, then these superficial views of marriage that lead so often to the divorce court can be done away with.

There are many who never see the spiritual importance of the home. There are some who even use the home as an excuse for spiritual superficiality. I have encountered untold dozens of people who use their parents as their excuse for failure to attend church. I've had a number of members of our church tell me, "Pastor, I won't be there Sunday. We're going to visit our parents." For what? For the sake of taking children back to see grandparents, using that as an excuse for failure to attend church? Would to God that all visitors who come to our city would come also into the house of God, and would to God that all of our people who visit in other cities on the Lord's Day would be found among the people of God. When company comes, that's an excuse to stay at home. We somehow believe that this is something that God approves. It's all right to stay at home as long as company is there. We use our homes incorrectly and sinfully, and indicate to the world that we don't think the home exerts a spiritual influence.

The home is a place of importance, but it is second in its importance to the kingdom of God. Jesus Christ said, "Seek ye *first* the kingdom of God." Now this is grammatically incorrect, and I'll tell you English teachers before I say it, but it is the only way I can express what I want to say. There can't be anything "firster" than first. You know what I'm talking about, don't you? "First" stands in a position of uniqueness. There is nothing "firster" than first. Now, it matters little or nothing what's second or third, or in any other lesser category, but it matters a great deal what is first. There is no home that can truly be a Christian home but that puts the kingdom of God first. If your home is a place of importance, it has importance and eternal significance because it has placed the Lord Christ in his proper position.

Children come to the place where they feel that Sunday is a day to go to visit grandparents. Why do so many take their families, lock, stock, and barrel, back to the parental home on the week-end? Why? I'll tell you. It's because of an insecurity those parents feel. They're afraid that they're not providing for their children what their parents provided for them. They take their children back to the parental home, hoping that the grandparents will be able to give to the grandchildren something that the grandparents gave to the sons and daughters. That's the way it works. Everything goes by the board when we go visiting, and those whom we visit are kept from being in the house of God because we've written and told them that we're coming. Isn't it strange? "Seek ye first the kingdom of God." Our homes become places of importance only when we get Jesus Christ in his proper place in the home.

A prominent sociologist said that only one home out of every four in America is a happy home. This was on the basis of his contact with people in counseling situations. One home out of every four is a happy home. The other three of those meet different fates. The second one ends in a divorce court. But the other two, said this sociologist, are not happy homes but stay together for reasons of economics or children, or something of the kind. What a commentary! One home out of every four in America today a happy home. Is it your home? Or is your home one of those little finger-shaking, name-calling arenas which has become a little hell on earth, where you go to fuss and fight and argue? Now what is your home? Is it a place of importance where love abounds because Jesus Christ occupies his rightful position, or is it something God never intended it to be? One of my great heartbreaks is the number of homes that are either breaking up or are on the rocks. Literally dozens of people have come to me and have called or contacted me because of marital difficulties. The most tragic word I hear spoken is, "There is no love left." Somebody has had a false concept of love and marriage.

Maybe marriage has been entered into too rapidly. You know, a seventeen year old isn't ready for marriage. I'm sorry to have to tell some of you high school students that. I'm sure it disappoints you. You may think you're the exception, but you're not. You're not emotionally mature enough for marriage at the age of seventeen. Now I know you're going to say, "Well, Grandpa and Grandma . . ." Yeah, I know that. They were cut out of a different bolt of cloth! They were different people entirely. They were people who dared to stand on their own two feet. Seventeen year olds today don't even intend to work for a living. They want somebody to give them a living. They want mamas and daddies to pass out the money whenever they need it. They want mamas and daddies to put them through college, with an automobile, with a furnished apartment, with plenty of spending money, and those are the marriages today that end in these divorce mills, running directly counter to the clear teaching of the Word of God. "What God has joined together, let not man put asunder."

Young people stand before a preacher in a holy hour and they pledge their vows one to the other, giving their sacred word, "until death do us part." Those same young people, a few months or a year or so later, stand very glibly in front of a judge as he pounds his gavel and says, "Divorce granted." Under heaven, have we raised a generation of liars, who don't even know the truth from falsehood, who don't have any concept of the value of their word?

Listen, my friend, don't you think when you are

seventeen or eighteen or nineteen that you can get
married and "everything's going to work out." It isn't.
Things don't work out—you work things out! The hard-
est job you'll ever have is the job of making a happy
home. It'll take 24 hour vigilance on your part and on
the part of the individual you marry. My friend, if
you're not careful in the selection of your marriage
partner, you've got a life of trouble ahead.

How are we going to do something about the divorce
rate? I'm not here to condemn those of you who are
divorced. I'm here to give our young people a warning.
This is serious business. It is no trial and error proposition. How are we going to teach our kids this? We teach
them by parental example. We teach them by creating
Christian homes, and making those homes stand for
what they ought to stand for; putting Jesus Christ in the
place of centrality in those homes. Then our homes are
places of importance; then they take a step toward an-
swering the problem of juvenile delinquency.

Homes are not only to be places of *importance,* according to the Word of God they're to be places of
          Instruction

There's a song in the musical, "South Pacific," originally a Broadway play with the lead sung by Mary Mar-
tin. We have a recording of that score at our house and
I like to listen to the music. There's one song that really
hit me—the truth that it has. It says "You've got to be
taught to hate." That's right. That's exactly right.
You've got to be taught to hate. You didn't come into

the world hating people of other races. If you hate them, somebody taught you to hate them.

But you know, just the reverse of that is true also. You've got to be taught to love. I don't like to disappoint our high school kids again, but there is no such thing as a "natural born lover." Some of you boys may think you are. I'm sure that's a rude jolt, and I hate to be the one to tell you, but there's no such thing as a natural born lover. You've got to be taught to love. There are a lot of parents who are literally stupid in their relationship to their children right at this point, and I say that advisedly. I hope that I'm not talking about too many of you. Parents show their stupidity and unfitness to have a family when they resign themselves and say, "Well, Preacher, I'm not going to insist that my child go to Training Union, or to prayer meeting. I'm going to wait until he gets big enough and let him make up his own mind." Listen, you! Wake up before it's too late. You'd better get busy teaching your child.

I talked to a person this week about his relationship to the church. I asked, "How old is your child?" and he told me. I said, "Do you know that in a matter of just a few years that child will be gone, and you'll have no further influence over that child?" When they get eighteen, or maybe nineteen, they're gone, gone, gone! They're off in college, they're married, They're away from home, and they're no longer under the influence of our homes. What are we going to do for them? Are we going to sit back and give up our responsibility by default? Are we going to say, "I'm not going to insist that my child do these things?"

Now if you're that kind of parent, then be consistent. Follow all the way through. Plow to the end of the row on that same philosophy. Let your child make up his own mind about what he's going to eat. I know some who would eat candy three times a day if their parents didn't insist that they do otherwise. They like sweets! But you know, God gives children to adults. At least physically they're adults, and they're supposed to have more sense than the children. God gave us intelligence that we might use it in rearing them. If we know that the kingdom of God is the place in which they are to center all of their hopes and ambitions for the future, let's be busy bringing them to the house of God and teaching our children what they ought to know. Our homes are places of instruction. If a child grows up to have an unchristian view of Sunday night, where did he learn it? Most of the time he learned it from indifferent parents who don't care what their children do on Sunday night. I think Dr. Lee was right. He said, "A lot of young people are more damned into this world than they are born into this world." It's something they can't do anything about because they didn't choose their parents. It's tragic, but true.

We need to instruct our children in the eternal verities of the Christian faith. We've got to teach boys and girls that the best things in life can't be bought by the coin of the realm. Why is it that kids hold up filling

stations and grocery stores and other places of business?
Why is it that they beat people up and take away their
money? Because all that they've ever heard in their
home is money, money, money, and they decide early
in life: "If I just get enough money, any way I can get
it, all my problems are solved." They learned it around
that dinner table where you argue about money, day
in and day out, every week that rolls around.

Somebody's going to have to teach our children the
way of salvation. Who's going to teach your child? Are
you going to wait until some Sunday School teacher
leads your boy or girl to Jesus? You may not be able to
witness to anybody else in all the world but, my friend,
you can win your own children to Christ. You'd better
be busy about it. I would take it as a slam against my
life, against my Christian profession, and against my
ministry if some sincere, dedicated Sunday School or
Training Union worker had the privilege and joy of
leading one of my children to accept Jesus. I would
count my life as a failure if I couldn't even win my own
children to Jesus Christ. But there are many parents
who sit back and let the Sunday School teacher claim
a trophy that the parent ought to claim for the sake of
Jesus. The reason more children aren't taught in the
homes is because some parents don't know the way of
salvation. Do you know that we have parents in this
community who are red-white-and-blue mad because
their children have trusted Jesus in the Sunday School
of this church? Brother, they can get mad! We're in

business for that purpose and for nothing else, and if you don't want your children taught the way of salvation, then they're in the wrong place. Get them out of the church of the Lord Jesus, for that's what we're here for. That's what we're here for whether or not you like it or believe it.

There's something else we had better teach our children in the home. We'd better teach our children a Christian concept of morality. God's Word has not changed. The immorality and sexual promiscuity of our day and time is a clear perversion of Christian teaching. Don't blame it on God, don't blame it on society! Somebody had better teach our boys and girls Romans 12:1, "I beseech you therefore brethren, by the mercies of God, that you present your bodies."—What? As stained, tarnished vessels? No! "As living sacrifices." There are some things that are saved for marriage. Do you hear me? There are some things that are reserved for marriage. And just because you've dabbled in that sin already is not an indication that this is right in the sight of God. It is wrong!

Homes need to rise up militantly to combat the insidious influences of the devil's crowd. Our boys and girls are being taught 24 hours a day by television industry and by the movie industry and by radio. Who's going to counteract those influences? Every time we look up, turn on the television, or listen to the radio, we are told that "beer belongs." Belongs where? Belongs in hell, that's where it belongs. It doesn't belong in the refrigerator of a child of God. I agree with Dr. Ramsey Pollard. I'd like to pile up all the beer, wine, and whiskey in the whole world and kick it to hell. That's where it belongs; that's where it came from, and that's where it takes people. Our homes are not what they ought to be, and somebody had better arouse us. We'd better wake up to the truth.

Our boys and girls are being taught on every hand, "Sow your wild oats while you're young and get them out of your system." Somebody's got to rise up and say, "I beseech you to present your body as a living sacrifice." Who's going to do it in your home? Who's going to tell your child the way of moral purity? Some day you young people will come to the marriage altar. You'll not want to know that the one that you're marrying is second-hand. But you have no more right to expect your wife to be pure than you have the right to be pure yourself. She has a right to expect something of you. Nobody wants a second-hand wife or a second-hand husband. Where are our boys and girls going to learn this? They'd better learn it from mamas and daddies who are spiritually alert and perceptive, and who make the home a place of instruction. Our world is a world that has gone haywire with sexual promiscuity, with unspeakable immorality; but Christian homes have got to retain their adherence to a biblical standard of morality and, in so doing, retain their own sanity. Our homes have got to be places of *importance* and places of *instruction,* but more than that, they've got

to be places of
> *Intercession*

I like the motto that our Catholic friends used several years ago: "Homes that pray together stay together." I believe that.

Robert Ingersoll, who was one of the most militant atheists and one of the most brilliant orators of another generation, once said that it was the first eight years of his life that made him what he was. He said, "How can a child be taught to pray with reverence, 'Our Father which art in heaven' when the only father that he knows is wilful, harsh, mean, stubborn, and unyielding?" It's a pretty good question, isn't it?

Dr. R. G. Lee, in a revival meeting in the church where I was pastor sometime ago, told an illustration that burned its way into my memory. He said a boy lay on a hospital bed dying. The members of his family had gathered around the bed. The parents were there with tears streaming silently down their cheeks. The boy seemingly was asleep, but he aroused himself, opened his eyes, and called for his father. His father immediately came to the side of the bed. He looked up into his father's face and he said, "Father, I understand that I'm not going to live long." The father, with tears running afresh said, "Son, that's true. As far as the medical men can tell us, life is not long." Then he said, "If that be true, Dad, I have one last request." His father immediately responded, "Son, anything, anything! Just name it." He replied, "Daddy when I die, I'd like to be

buried down behind the house by the lot gate." His
father looked at him and said, "Son, that's a rather
strange request. I don't know why you want this, but
if that's what you want that's what will be done. But
why is this?" He said, "Because, Daddy, I know that
every morning when you go out to the field to work,
you go through that gate. When you come home every
day at noon for dinner you come back through that
gate. You go out after dinner, back out into the field to
do your work, and you come in through that same gate
late in the afternoon. Every time you pass through that
gate, I want you to look over there and say to yourself:
'There lie the bones of a son of mine in Hell today, who
never heard his daddy pray.' " I wonder how many
there are in hell today who raise that plaintive wail—"I
never heard my daddy pray?" Our homes have got to
be places of *intercession*.

5

WHEN TROUBLE COMES

As I've stood in the pulpit over the years and looked out across a veritable sea of faces, I have tried to be mindful of individual as well as corporate need. Some sermons are directed primarily to community needs that exist within the state or nation, or perhaps some world need. Other sermons are directed to the fact that there are individuals in the congregation who have a specific need.

There are not many families in our church that have escaped heartache and trouble in a period of seven years. Yet I still meet members of my church for the first time when trouble comes in their families.

There was a popular song when I was a teen-ager entitled, "Into Each Life Some Rain Must Fall." It was made popular on a recording by a group called the Ink Spots. Those men could sing beautifully and harmoniously together. That song was number one on the Hit Parade for a long time. "Into each life some rain must fall." There's no doubt about the truth in that. Whether it be the high school student who has just lost the all-important school election; or the widow dressed in black who stands and surveys the loneliness and desolation of a once happy and cheerful home; or the grieving father whose soul has been pierced by the serpent's tooth of an ungrateful son; or a sorrowing mother who weeps silently over a tiny white casket that contains the lifeless form of the object of her affections and the center of her hopes; or maybe the brokenhearted person who has been outraged at the disloyalty of a trusted friend; or possibly distraught, distracted parents sitting in the gloom of what the world calls disgrace; whoever you are, whatever your trouble, I call you to remember that God never promised you exemption from it, he rather promised victory in it.

I want to say three things about trouble. First, I want to point out that it is objective, then that it's ordinary, and finally, that it is an opportunity.

Objective

Some of our troubles are self made. On occasion we get in trouble because we talk too much. Sometimes we get in trouble because we overextend ourselves financially and find ourselves in a financial bind. Actually, the gravest troubles life brings are objective and impersonal. They are not things you have brought about by your actions.

The afflictions of Job were not the result of sin. He had not grievously rebelled against God. That was not the reason for his suffering, but rather his afflictions were designed to prove him, to put his faith to the test, and show the world his unswerving loyalty to almighty God.

So often people ask, "Why did God do this? Why did God take my loved one? Why does God allow the injustices and inequities of war to continue? Why does God not put a stop to hatred, racial prejudice, the social inequalities we see, to sickness and cancer? Why does God not stop sorrow, pain, and heartache?" Those questions come to me every week. They are questions that have plagued the human race since the beginning of time. I don't begin to profess to have an answer, but I have a suggestion. The suggestion has been made that instead of making trouble a question mark, let's make it an exclamation point. Let's not relate our troubles to theology, asking "Why did God do this?" Let's relate our troubles to doxology and in the midst of trouble praise God! I believe that's what Paul meant in our text. "God works all things together for good to those who love him, who are the called according to his purpose."

On a recent occasion in a soul-winning technique study I dealt with this question briefly. So many people ask, "Why does God allow sin? Why doesn't God clean out the graft and the corruption in government? Why doesn't God bring things like this to a halt?" I pause to ask myself, "If God were to put a stop to sin, prejudice, injustice, to iniquity of every kind, where would he stop?" He certainly could not stop short of you and me, and if God were to put a stop to all sin that would pretty well clean us out, wouldn't it? There wouldn't be anybody left if God were to stop death and sickness and pain and sin and all of these unpleasant things, for all of us are contributors. If God cleaned it up, he would have to clean us out along with it.

The apostle Paul knew as much about trouble as any man who ever walked on this earth, save our Lord himself. Paul had been beaten, both with a rod and a whip. He had been stoned; he had been jailed, he had been shipwrecked; he had been cursed, mocked, spat upon and abused by those who were formerly his Jewish allies. Yet we find the faith of Paul to be of the triumphant sort, for his faith claimed the victory and shouted the doxology. Paul is the very one who wrote, "God works all things together for good to those who love him, who are the called according to his purpose." Paul gloried in his privilege of suffering for Christ, and he let suffering work to the honor and glory of Jesus, whom he loved and lived to serve. He didn't whine and complain but shouted in triumph, "There hath no temptation taken you but such as is common to man: but God is faithful, who will not suffer you to be tempted above that which ye are able; but will with the temptation also make way to escape, that ye may be able to bear it." Many times you have heard an old-timer say in a day of trouble, "I know God won't put more on me than I can bear." I've heard it many times. This person is simply reiterating the promise Paul recorded that was proven in his own experience. There's nothing that can happen to you but that God will give you strength to bear up under it and use it ultimately for his honor and glory.

The loss of your loved one, the loss of your health, the loss of your job or fortune is not some devious manner God has of punishing you. It rather is an objective experience that affords you the opportunity of revealing your faith and the sufficiency of God's grace. When trouble comes, pause to thank God for counting you faithful and giving you that opportunity to honor him. So first, trouble is objective. That is, it doesn't come because you have sinned. Job's troubles didn't. Jesus cleared this up when asked about a blind man, "Who sinned, this man or his parents?" Jesus replied, "Neither one. This whole situation exists so that God might be honored." That's true in your life and mine. Secondly, remember that troubles are

Ordinary

By that I mean you can expect trouble to come. When it comes, trouble can be like a diving board. Many of you are parents. You've gone through the trauma of teaching your children to swim. I've had that experience four times! I know whereof I speak! You've all seen the little child walk to the end of the diving board, stop, look around fearfully, shout to his parents at the top of his voice, "Hey Daddy, watch me; look at me, Mommy." Making a horrible face and holding his nose he jumps in, feet first, with a glorious splash. Then you've seen the mature swimmer stride up gracefully, soar into the air and dive neatly into the water, scarcely making a ripple.

People react to trouble like that. You find the immature Christian, when trouble comes, shouting for everyone to hear, "Look at me, look at me. No one has suffered like I've suffered." Making a horrible face and acting as if God were dead, he goes through the experience trying to call attention to himself. Then you've seen the mature Christian, when trouble comes, accept it as an opportunity to glorify God and use the trouble as a springboard to lift him into greater proximity to the throne of grace.

Think of the great and the small who live with trouble! Most of us think that if we could command a vast fortune all of our problems would be solved. On occasion we may have been prone to envy the Kennedy family, reputed to be worth many millions of dollars. Have you stopped to think of the trouble that family has which money cannot solve? Three sons have been lost in the service of their country, two in political office and one serving the United States in a military uniform. In addition to that kind of trouble, the Kennedy family has a retarded daughter who has been in a home for retarded persons for years on end. Think of the trouble that they have for which even a vast fortune cannot compensate.

The greatest preacher produced by Southern Baptists, in my judgment, in all the years of our existence, was Dr. George W. Truett, a true prophet of God. His life and ministry stand as a monument to the Lord Jesus Christ. Early in life Dr. Truett was in a hunting accident with his closest friend, the chief of police of Dallas,

Texas, and in the accident the gun was discharged and his best friend died as a result. Yet George Truett carried that burden through his lifetime and used it as a springboard for a closer walk with God. Those who knew him best said it was that experience which gave him the mellow faith he had, that gave him the compassion and pathos revealed in his life in his relationship to other human beings. Trouble is ordinary. It comes to all, whether the rich or the poor, the well known or the obscure.

Trouble can be a wise instructor if we are willing to learn. Many of the greatest lessons in life can be learned while in the valley of the shadow. No one can truly know God intimately until trouble comes, and when overwhelmed and deluged, deep calleth unto deep.

That was the experience David had in the twenty-third Psalm. When the pastures were green and the waters still, David said, "He leadeth me, he restoreth my soul." When the stormclouds of trouble began to gather and the valley of the shadow was near, he cried, "Thou art with me, thy rod and thy staff they comfort me." The change in pronoun indicated the more intimate relationship when trouble came. People who have it easy and never suffer are usually giddy and superficial, for it's still true that "all sunshine makes a desert." We ought to know, living in this part of Texas. Unless rain falls in our geographical area frequently, there'll be nothing but desert. When trouble comes, just know that it is an ordinary part of living, for the

Bible says, "Man's days are few and full of trouble."
Then finally, trouble is an

Opportunity

The grandest opportunity you will ever have to glorify God and prove your faith is in the hour of stress and
storm. When everything's rosy, the pastures are green,
and the waters still, you can sing lustily, "Praise God
from whom all blessings flow." Pagans say, "Oh, yeah,
who couldn't sing that when everything goes well?" It's
different when you have an experience like eight of
nine brothers who stood by the bedside of their dying
mother and watched their beloved parent slip down
the cold, caustic corridor of death. Without any
prompting, simultaneously they burst into the doxology, singing with broken voices and with tears
streaming down their cheeks, "Praise God from whom
all blessings flow." Then a pagan world will sit up and
take notice, for you're revealing your faith is secure and
will see you through a time of trouble.

When the crepe is on the door, when the job is gone
and the health is lost, or when the fortune has vanished,
then dear friends, you have a golden opportunity to
glorify God. Trouble may be listed on the world's books
as a liability, but in the Christian system of bookkeeping
it goes down as an asset. Life's greatest opportunities
are often seen through the telescope of a tear.

If we rise from a sickbed without new gratitude to
God for life and health, we have suffered in vain. Unless
we stand by the quiet, cold form of a departed loved

one to have rekindled within us a new sympathy for every other mourner, we have sorrowed in vain. Each time we walk beside an open grave, we must let the lilies speak their resurrection promise, or we have grieved in vain.

A Christian blacksmith many years ago had great troubles. Skeptics questioned him about this. They expressed amazement. They asked, "You're a Christian; how do you explain all of these troubles you're having?" With a smile he replied, "I've answered this to my own satisfaction. I'll be happy to try to answer it to yours." Taking an everyday illustration he said, "Here at my blacksmith shop I take a piece of iron, heat it to a white heat, and strike it to see if it will take temper. Next, I plunge it into the water to change the temperature, and then back it goes into the fire. If it will take temper, I put it on the anvil and hammer it into a useful article." He continued, "If that piece of iron will not take temper, I throw it out the back door onto the scrap heap." He stated, "I've asked the Lord to put me in the fire, put me in the water, put me on the anvil, anything that needs be, but O Father, for Christ's sake, don't throw me on the scrap heap."

A murderer is punished for the crime he has committed, but a child is disciplined for the good that he can do in the future. That's the attitude Christians have toward troubles. Going through a period of troubles simply fits us and qualifies us to better serve the risen Christ.

Romans 8:28 (RSV) assures us that "We know that in everything God works for good with those who love him, who are called according to his purpose."

6

INGREDIENTS FOR HAPPINESS

I recently asked a young couple about to be married what they wanted most out of life. They thought for a moment and then stated the one thing they most wanted was happiness. I think you would agree with me that happiness is a worthy goal, and yet most human beings never face the fact that happiness is not in circumstances, but happiness is within us. Happiness is not something beautiful that we behold with the eye like a rainbow, nor is it something that we can feel like the wonderful warmth of a fire on a cold, winter night. Happiness is something far different than that.

There was a catchy little pop tune not long ago that had a number of stanzas all beginning with "happiness is." In that song, which I enjoyed as much as you, we learned that happiness is one thing for a baseball player, it's another thing for a parent or other individuals. Invariably these suggestions had to do with things, and I've come to remind us that's not "where it's at." It's somewhere else. Things do not offer happiness to human beings. Not even Jefferson and those boys with him who helped write the Constitution guaranteed happiness as an inalienable right. The men who framed the Constitution of the United States rather guaranteed the right to the pursuit of happiness, for they had enough wisdom to know they couldn't offer happiness to humanity—it is that quality of life individually acquired.

Happiness is not a passive matter. It is ours to seek and comes as the result of certain activity. I'm inclined to believe that is the reason our Lord put such great emphasis on personal involvement. Throughout his ministry Jesus Christ called on people to become involved and get active. The basic demand of the Kingdom is: "If any man would come after me, let him deny himself and take up his cross and follow me." This is activity. This is involvement and I have come to share with you my own deep conviction that you'll never know happiness until you know active involvement. I would like to suggest three ingredients that I believe are integral parts of happiness. These are accept, agree, and applaud.

Accept

first of all. The starting point is when one accepts Jesus Christ and his manner of life. To some of you this may be repugnant, for you simply cannot convince yourself that happiness could ever come through acquiescence to the will of another. You've already convinced yourself that happiness comes when you do it your way, when you live your life without any restrictions from the outside, when you never accept any demands or commands from another person.

As strange as it may sound, happiness comes when you accept the will of Jesus Christ for your life. Those who have retired at an early age will tell you that life becomes absolutely frustrating when one does not have planned activities resulting in service to someone else. Those who enjoy retirement and who continue to know the zest of living after retirement plan premeditatively to remain active. These are the ones who continue to serve. Happiness comes through service and it takes no prophet to remind us that the only lasting service we can render is service for Jesus Christ through his kingdom's program. The only eternal institution on the face of the earth is the church of the Lord Jesus Christ, for which he died and which one day he's coming into the world to claim for himself as his holy bride: his church without spot or wrinkle.

True service centers in this area, yet we are forced to conclude that there are those who have accepted Jesus Christ genuinely but nevertheless remain unhappy. Have you ever known an unhappy Christian? I have, and there's nothing in all the world more heartbreaking, for this is roughly equivalent to a man dying of thirst as he stands on the bank of a mighty river. How could it be? That is like a man who dies of hunger as he stands with his hands full of bread. How can one be an unhappy Christian?

I think we must agree that there are some additional steps that have to be taken after one accepts Jesus Christ, for it then becomes necessary that one accept himself. Most of us try to live on the instalment plan, at least where happiness is concerned. The philosophy of life by which we live centers in the two little words "when I." Have you not talked with people like this, and have you not lived in that atmosphere yourself? "When I" get my education, then; "when I" finish my military obligations; "when I" get married; "when I" get my debts paid; "when I" get that promotion; "when" summer vacation comes, and we never realize that our unhappiness centers in unrealized dreams. As long as we live in this atmosphere of unreality and consign everything to the future, we'll never be happy today. That's the instalment plan of living and there has never been anyone to experience happiness living by that plan. You'll never know happiness today if you're referring all of your activities and responsibilities to the future.

One of the phenomena of our day is the rapid rise in suicides in the United States. I don't have the answer to this problem, but I know this: A person who takes his own life is a person who has come to question the worthwhileness of it all. He has convinced himself that life is just not worth continuing. In despair such a person wants out. I want to say something to you who are alive. If you question the value of life and if you've ever wondered seriously if it's worth it, if you've ever put any question marks over your own existence, it may well be that you've never discovered what life's all about. If you don't think life is worthwhile, it may well be that you have set some unworthy goals for yourself or that you have no goals at all. Dear friend, that is not God's fault; that's your fault. As the poet said,

> Life is real! Life is earnest!
>   And the grave is not its goal;
> Dust thou art, to dust returneth,
>   Was not spoken of the soul.

Yet, if we are to know happiness, we must come to the point where we are willing to accept other people. It's man's individuality that makes the world an interesting and challenging place in which to live. God has given each human a personality unlike any other on the face of the earth. God has given us particular abilities so that each one contributes his own specialty to society. No one else can contribute your specialty.

Ralph Waldo Emerson said, "Don't try to make other people over into a copy of yourself, for God knows, and you should too, that one person like you is all the world can stand." Thank you, Mr. Emerson, for reminding us of that fact!

Most of us are born with a congenital desire to make people conform to our standards. Friend, you'll never know happiness until you're willing to accept the individuality of other human beings. I'm not talking about moral issues, I'm not talking about those areas in life where God's Word has a clear and positive admonition. I'm talking about those areas in life where morality is not involved, where individuals act in different ways from other persons. Until you're willing to accept

other people and cease this nefarious practice of trying
to make them over into your own mold, you'll never
know happiness. When we reach the point of being
able to accept people as they are, and love them in the
same way that God loves us, in spite of glaring weaknesses and apparent inconsistencies, until we reach
that point we'll never know true happiness. You'll
never be happy as long as you are trying to remake the
world and particularly certain other individuals with
whom you live in close proximity. When we accept
others, even as God has accepted us, then we move a
long step in the direction of happiness.

This ingredient is to accept—accept Jesus and his will
and way for our lives—accept ourselves with all of our
sin and rascality and stupidity, and understand that we
have value because Jesus died for us, and if there's
nothing about our lives to commend us, that one thing
makes us worthwhile. Then we must be willing to accept other people for the same reason—that Christ died
for them, too—and we ought to periodically rejoice and
thank God that he didn't make us all alike. The second
ingredient we need to mix into this potion is

Agree

In Amos 3:3 the question is asked, "Can two walk
together except they be agreed?" The answer is not
given but the implication is negative. No, two can't
walk together except they be agreed. If they're not
agreed, one will go in one direction and one in the
other direction. To walk together implies agreement.

The same truth in different words is found in Paul's writing where he admonished believers not to be unequally yoked together with unbelievers. Since home is vitally connected with happiness, agreement must begin in the home. That's the starting point, and there can be no other.

One excellent word of advice to those who are involved in the business of homemaking is this: "Never shout in the house unless the house is on fire." I was visiting in a home not long ago and when I finally got the husband and the wife to stop shouting at each other I was able to talk with them. Of course, that took about an hour and twenty minutes, but finally we were able to talk as grownups.

It has also been said when there is shouting in the home, the house *is* on fire and it's the marriage that's going up in smoke.

We ought to be in agreement in the home in regard to matters of a spiritual nature, for when we disagree in the realm of the things of the spirit, that disagreement among parents results in the production of spiritual schizophrenics among children. Where a father has one set of convictions and a mother has another and the children are torn between the two, what is the result? You know what the result is! Children are divided asunder and have no clear-cut convictions. If a mother, for instance, has deep convictions regarding the church and regular support of its services and the father has none or is antagonistic, the result is discord, a lock of agreement.

There must be agreement as to what constitutes a happy relationship. Father may have one idea of a happy relationship while mother has a different one. It may be the father's idea that happiness means being left alone. He comes in at night as the lord and master of the household, plops himself down in a chair, wanting no responsibility, wanting no one to say anything to him, just wanting to be left alone. He thinks that's happiness.

Maybe the wife in that home thinks happiness is a sharing relationship in which the father takes his rightful place as a part of the team, and because of this disagreement they draw farther and farther apart until divorce or separation, and the children are left to be raised by in-laws or loved ones or maybe a foster home. There has got to be agreement as to what constitutes a happy relationship or else the result will be a lifetime of anguish.

Some people think this happy relationship can be brought. They think it has to do with a house in a certain section of town, with the interior decor designed by certain interior decorators, with furniture bought from certain leading stores and with the last word in appliances and things money can buy. It is frightening to know the number of people who have equated this with happiness. Someone put it this way, "Success is getting what you want; happiness is wanting what you get." Friend, there's a big difference. It's practically impossible for you to be happy if you're married to an unhappy person.

The story is told of a king who was stricken with a rare malady. The physicians could offer no help and finally there was a rather queer character in the king's court, a soothsayer, who came with the awesome pronouncement that the king would be cured if he could wear the shirt of a happy man for one day. Grasping at straws and having no hope offered from the physicians, they set out over the kingdom searching for a happy man. Alas, when he was found, he had no shirt!

Look back over the years of your life. What were your happiest years? If they were any other than this present moment you probably would say that they were the years when you had little of this world's goods, when you and the other members of your family were working together as a team for the accomplishment of certain agreed upon goals. Where is happiness? Is it "having it made" as far as the bank or your broker is concerned?

Have you heard the story of the young executive who was sitting behind his new desk when one of his old friends walked in? He had just gotten this new position of affluence and wanted to impress everyone. When the friend walked in and sat down he said, "Excuse me for a moment." He picked up the telephone and called his secretary and said, "Get me my regular broker on the phone." And she, not knowing that he was trying to impress someone said, "Stock or pawn?" Now I'll give you a few minutes and you will catch that. Look back over your life. What were your happiest years? Were they the years when you had the most money in your pocket? Probably not. Probably not, but the years when you were working for something you knew was worthwhile.

Purify your purpose. Focus your faith. Jesus said on one occasion, "For this cause, came I into the world." Why are you here? Where are you going now that you are here? What is your purpose in life? I read somewhere that happiness is like perfume that you can't pour on someone else without getting a few drops on yourself. I think that's good. If you want to be happy, get to work trying to make somebody else happy and you'll find that happiness is on the inside. While you're trying to pour this perfume on someone else, you're getting it all over yourself! Accept first, and then agree. There's a final ingredient for happiness and that is

Applaud

I think of the three this probably is the most neglected and least utilized. One day a man observed a woman boarding a bus with ten children. He looked at her for a moment and asked, "Are all these yours, or are you going on a picnic?" She looked at him and snapped, "They're all mine and it's no picnic."

Now for my male audience, I want to remind all of us that it's no picnic to keep house, cook meals, iron clothes, run a taxicab for the children, and to try to balance a food budget. Yet there's another side to that coin, for it's also nerve racking and exhausting to face the daily grind of the business world, to constantly live with sometimes unfair competition and inner-office rivalries, to wonder in the midst of ever increasing costs and spiraling taxes how one can feed and clothe and educate his family. The point is, life is demanding for both the husband and wife, and the least that we can do in the home relationship is to show a little appreciation for one another. Take time out to applaud, to say thank you. Say frequently, "You did a good job, I appreciate what you have done, and what you're doing."

Perhaps the greatest thing that parents do for children is to love each other as adults. It's in the love of parents for each other that children develop their sense of security. It's significant, I believe, that in creation, when God created Eve, he took a rib from Adam's side. She did not come from Adam's head to be dominated by him, she did not come from Adam's feet to be walked upon, but from his side that she might be equal to him, from under his arm that she might be protected by him, and from near his heart that she might be loved by him. In other words, this is a two-way street. If we are to know happiness, there must be a time in our lives when we take time out to say thank you to someone who is richly deserving of that accolade.

Is there someone to whom you ought to say thank you today? Maybe your wife, perhaps your husband, or could it be a parent or some close friend who has stood by you through thick and thin? Maybe it's a Sunday

School teacher who has challenged you to grow in the Christian faith. Maybe it's a neighbor who through long years has shown friendship and appreciation. Is there someone to whom you today ought to express sincere gratitude?

I believe for many of us it would be Jesus Christ, who has done so much for us. Maybe we have taken him for granted; maybe we have overlooked our obligations to him; maybe we have just shrugged off our responsibilities as Christians. I want to remind you that you show your love and gratitude to him through his church and the work of his Kingdom here on earth. If you love him and are grateful to him, you'll want to show that love and gratitude by taking your stand in service for him.

7

FACING OUR FEARS

Psalm 34:4

The angelic message to a group of shepherds on a Judean hillside was, "Fear not, for behold I bring you good tidings of great joy which shall be to all people." The angel of God, speaking to Joseph the husband of Mary, said, "Fear not to take unto thee Mary, thy wife." The angel who spoke to Zacharias, the priest, said, "Fear not, Zacharias, for thy prayer has been heard." To Mary, the earthly mother of our Lord, the angel of God said, "Fear not, for thou hast found favor in the sight of the Lord." At least six times in the gospel narrative, our Lord Jesus Christ said, "Fear not."

It occurs to me that the Christian gospel can be applied in a very direct way in the area of human fear. If you take your concordance and trace every use of this word in the Old and New Testaments, you'll find that the admonition of God to his people in Old Testament times as well as the warning of Jesus Christ to his followers in New Testament times was, "Fear not." That admonition rings in our ears. The presence of God in our lives forbids fear if we are to live joyously and victoriously for him.

On one occasion during his earthly ministry the Lord

Jesus said that he had come to bring deliverance to the captives. Some of those in our day who are the most pitiable captives of all are held in the grip of debilitating and enslaving fears. Are you a fearful person?

Our age has been characterized in a wide variety of ways. For instance, we have been called the "space age." In other quarters ours has been designated "the thermo-nuclear age." Still others like to refer to this day and generation as "the scientific age." There are truths to be found in all of these, yet it seems to me there is one categorization which is far more apt and universal than any of the others. In a real sense ours is an age of fear. I read some statistics recently stating the number of tons of aspirin consumed by the American people every 24 hours. I hesitate to say what my mind is telling me that number was. It was so fantastic that I found it hard to believe. Can you imagine how many of those little white pills it would take to make a ton? Surely ours is an age of fear.

In the minds of thinking people there is the ever-present possibility of World War III, overshadowed by a mushroom-shaped cloud. That ought to cause even the most superficial persons to pause and think. There are others living each day with a dreadful fear of personal involvement in the war in Southeast Asia. That fear is real in the lives of Americans as well as others in different parts of the world. Fears possess us today.

Our fears sometimes center in the matter of finances or our lack of money. Often we are fearful that what money we have will be taken away by the constantly eroding influence of inflation, or that maybe the little nest egg that has been tucked away in stocks and bonds will be lost by a decline of the stock market. Maybe the fear that grips our hearts with cold fingers is a fear of job security or a lack of it. Perhaps we're concerned about our health and we're looking toward the next appointment with the doctor with trembling and deep apprehension, fearful of what the outcome of the tests might be.

Still others are fearful over their lack of acceptance by their peers. This is particularly true of young people. One of the fears besetting youth is a fear of not being liked by their contemporaries.

Others are fearful of old age. If we set wrong goals for ourselves in life, old age is feared like a skeleton in the closet, a spectre looming over us every breath we breathe and every day we live.

There are untold millions of people who are fearful about salvation today, not knowing whether they have ever been born again. With these question marks they carry a heavy burden. Fear besets us all. What can a Christian do in regards to his fears? How is a Christian to react when fear sets in? I have some suggestions I'd like to share with you. They are three in number. I would suggest in the first place we *expose* them, in the second place *expel* them, and in the third place *expect* God's power and blessings.

Expose

Of all of the emotions that have been a part of the pattern of human behavior, fear probably has the most insidious power to make us do what we ought not to do and to keep us from doing what we ought to do. Isn't it a shame that fear works so conversely?

Fear is not the figment of the imagination, it's a very real emotion. Yet to know it's reality and be able to gauge something of its effect on our lives is not enough. All of us know about fear. All of us know that fear makes us do certain things that we know we should not do and leave undone some things that should have been accomplished.

Remember Adam. When God caught up with Adam, he said, "I was afraid and I hid myself." This characteristic is still found in the lives of humans thousands of years after Adam and Eve. When we are fearful, when we have uncertainties about our relationship to God, our tendency is to run and hide.

There are some of you reading this chapter who are hiding from God. You have talents you're afraid to put to use for Jesus. Maybe your fear is due to your inconsistent Christian life. Maybe you have a fear of failure—suppose I were to try and not succeed? Your fear has made you hide from God and you have proven in so doing that you are after the similitude of Adam.

From the very earliest moments of recorded history, fear and sin have walked in perfect cadence. When we sin and are swept by a sense of guilt and fear, we become more fearful and begin to run. When we consider Adam, as detached as we are from his situation, we rightly conclude it would have been far better for Adam to stop, evaluate his actions, confess his sin, and ask God's forgiveness. Most of us have 20/20 hindsight, and we exercise it in regard to Adam. When we find ourselves in a similar position, having drifted far from God, having sinned against God, having failed to fulfil God's purpose for our lives, rather than pausing to confess our sins and seek forgiveness, like Adam we run!

Forgiveness is an indispensable quality in dispelling fear. The Bible says, "If we confess our sins he is faithful and just to forgive our sins and to cleanse us from all unrighteousness." That passage reminds us that if forgiveness comes, sin must be exposed and confessed. You can't find forgiveness by concealing sin. Only through exposure can forgiveness and pardon come. Fears will be dispelled on the basis of pardon from God.

Have you ever been awakened late at night by a strange noise? Out of a dead sleep have you suddenly been brought into wide-awake consciousness and know that some noise had awakened you? If that has happened, the chances are that cold fear gripped your heart as you started to imagine all sorts of things in an effort to identify the strange sound.

I had this experience recently when my family was away and I was in that very large home by myself. I suddenly was wide awake. I knew that there was a strange noise that had awakened me and I had no idea what it was. I lay quietly for a moment, waiting to hear it again, and trying to identify it. In just a moment I heard it and quickly, almost instantaneously, a half-dozen things ran through my mind and all of them were bad! As I lay there, I reminded myself that I was a grown man. When I did this I got up, walked out into the hall, and stood there waiting for the sound. In a moment I heard it again. It happened that it was a windy night, and the wind was blowing through the attic causing that disappearing stairway to bump. Now I had that "bump" figured out a half-dozen different ways, but none of them had anything to do with a disappearing stairway. When I found out what it was, I turned on the lights and stood there. As I watched for a while I thought how silly I was! If I had not exposed that fear, I probably would have lost a good night's sleep. I doubt if I could have ever gone back to sleep until I had discovered what that noise was and brought my fear out into the open. I felt a little foolish when I identified it, and frankly I was not a little relieved.

* * *

What are your fears? Get them out in the open, expose them and when they have been exposed to yourself, expose them to God in open confession and receive his grace. Watch fear disappear under this kind of procedure. When fears are brought out where we can focus and clarify them, they can be seen in their proper light and in most cases there is no reason to be afraid! Now the second step. After you expose, it is necessary to

Expel

One of the most precious promises found in the Book is this: "Perfect love casteth out fear." Over a century ago a great preacher named Talmadge preached his famous sermon entitled, "The Expulsive Power of a New Affection." He based it on this text, "Perfect love casteth out fear." Paul, the incomparable apostle said, "Now abideth faith, hope, love but the greatest of these is love." I've reminded us of these verses to underscore the fact that love is a greater power than fear, and if fear is to be expelled, something more powerful must expel it.

Love and fear stand at opposite extremes, just like the North Pole and the South Pole marking the extremities of this earth. The significant thing is, the closer you draw to the North Pole the farther you are from the South Pole. The closer you come to the South Pole the farther you are from the North Pole. This is precisely true with love and fear. The closer you get to one the farther you are from the other. "Perfect love casteth out fear."

For many people, service rendered in the kingdom of God is based on fear. Now that is one motive for Christian service. Some people serve God out of fear, but let me hasten to remind you that though it is *a* motive, it is the lowest and least of all. Our service for Christ ought to be prompted by love, for we love because he first loved us. Our Lord said, "If you love me, keep my commandments." This way the world can know that we love Jesus Christ, if we keep his commandments. That's the one thing the world looks at us to discover. The big question in their minds is, "Does he obey Jesus?" If we obey Jesus, they can see a difference in our lives. If we love Jesus, we will be obedient to him.

How is it we can expel fear after having exposed it? Let's hear what Jesus had to say on the subject, and I believe this applies here. "Thou shalt love the Lord thy God with all thy heart, soul, mind and strength." Observe the inclusiveness of this. It includes the totality of human personality; the heart, the mind, the soul, the strength. If we love Jesus Christ with that sort of devotion, there is nothing left to be afraid of. There is no physical fear that can bother us if we love him with all of our strength. There is no mental apprehension that can cause us undue concern because our minds are focused and centered upon him. The way to expel fear is to follow the command of Jesus.

The love of God is to pervade every aspect of our being. Our minds are to be subservient to him. We are to make Jesus Christ the center pole of our thinking, fitting everything else in life, every other mental pursuit, to the centrality of Jesus Christ. If there is ever a seeming discrepancy between what Jesus said and what others say, we follow Jesus! You don't have any fears when you put Christ in that position. When Christ holds the reins of lordship over your mind, there's no room for fear.

Jesus said, "Ye shall know the truth and the truth shall make you free." How can you be liberated from your fears? By knowing the truth. But I'm glad Jesus didn't leave "truth" to our definition. Jesus defined truth when he said, "I am the truth." When you begin at that point you've got the right foundation. When you begin at some other point you'll never get the right foundation. He is it. He is the truth of God revealed in human form and when our minds accept that, when he becomes the center pole in our thought processes, everything else falls into its proper place. Truth is not some nebulous, elusive, hard-to-define matter, for Christ has defined it. He is the One who frees us; he is the One who liberates us from fears; he is the One who gives zest, tang, and thrill to daily living. When we place him in the proper position and love him with all our hearts, minds, souls, and strength, then our fears fade and vanish away.

Fear often sweeps us when the anchors upon which we have depended slip and prove unreliable. Maybe you have some anchors that have held to this point, yet the time will come when you'll discover those anchors are not to be trusted. When that time comes, if you've depended on your physical strength and health, if you've depended upon a large bank roll or your nest egg of savings, if you've depended upon the company for which you work or the American government to insure there'll be no recession or depressions, if you've depended upon the wrong thing, when that erroneous, falacious, not-to-be trusted anchor slips, then your heart will be gripped with fear. Like a house of cards or dominoes, when one falls, all fall.

There are people in our city for whom life seems to be closing in. More and more they're gripped by the coldness of their fears. The songwriter had a word to say on that subject when he wrote, "In times like these you need a Savior, in times like these you need an anchor, be very sure, be very sure, your anchor holds and grips the solid rock." And then the song states this rock is Jesus, he's the One! If you're depending upon anyone or anything other than Jesus, who is the Truth, then your anchor will not hold when the winds of adversity blow. If you're anchored to this rock, Jesus, your anchor and rock will dispel your fears. Now there's a final step and that is to

Expect

We're probably the busiest people who ever lived. We have more leisure time than any generation has ever had, and yet we are busier than any other generation. Undoubtedly we're all big wheels because all of us are going around in circles! The all too frequent results of our busy-ness is shallowness. Did you get this? The all too frequent result of our busy-ness is shallowness!

Genesis 3:8 speaks eloquently to our need. The record says Adam and Eve, walking in the cool of the day, heard the voice of God. Doesn't that say something to you? Can't you picture it? Walking in the cool of the day—what could be more relaxing, more invigorating, than to take a stroll in the cool of the day. It was under those circumstances they heard God speaking to them.

Our lives deepen and our love for Christ matures when we take time out to tune up. No musician spends all of his time in concert. No orchestra plays indefinitely without taking time to tune the instruments and get in harmony.

Someone suggested in a quip I read that we're like an old shoe, all worn out except the tongue. How apt a description.

We've been deluded by the phrase, "Falling in love." Most of us have fallen prey to the idea of "love at first sight." Not so! Don't you believe it! Where you can show me one person who fell in love at first sight, I'll show you a thousand who've learned what love is in a slow, yet ever-growing process. Love isn't something made up like instant tea. It isn't something like this instant cornbread one can buy in little corn kits and whip up instantly. Love comes slowly. We have to be taught to love. A motto of one of our first missionaries was, "Expect great things from God, attempt great things for God."

Dear friends, don't think of your life only in terms of activities. If you do, if you associate life with your busy-ness then naturally you are going to fear old age.

If you've come to find that life has more to offer than activity, then you can grow old gracefully.

Develop and guard your quiet time every day. That

is the time when you get alone with God and with his Word. If you don't have such a time you're missing one of the real blessings of life and foregoing one of your opportunities to dispel fears. I have a friend who signs his letters to me, "Keep looking up." I like that. It's a reminder to me and to all that our expectations exceed what this world has to offer, and that he who loves us with an everlasting love is coming some day soon. Keep looking up. What's left to be afraid of?

8

THE HOLY SPIRIT AND YOU

Acts 1:8

Jesus said, "Ye shall receive power after the Holy Ghost has come upon you, and ye shall be witnesses unto me in Jerusalem, in Judea and in Samaria and unto the uttermost part of the earth."

I believe you would agree that the Holy Spirit is the least understood of the Trinity. We talk a great deal about God the Father and God the Son. We preach many sermons that extol the virtues and characteristics of the Father God. Our ministry seems to focus upon the life and teachings of the Lord Jesus Christ, yet little emphasis is given upon the One to whom we look for spiritual health and strength in this life. If you take a hymnal and search its pages, you'll find hymns written about the ministry and Person of the Holy Spirit can almost be numbered on the fingers of one hand. We give little mention to him in song or in sermon.

In the King James translation he is often referred to as the Holy Ghost. Frankly, the word "ghost" does not have a spiritual orientation. In the minds of most of us, when we say ghost we think of Hallowe'en and some-one trying to play a trick on someone else with a bed-sheet over his head. When we put holy and ghost together, it just does not speak to our spiritual need. Maybe this is one of the reasons we have turned in the wrong direction.

All of this is a paradox for we are as dependent in the spiritual life upon the Holy Spirit as we are in the physical life upon breath. The Greek word *pneuma,* or spirit, can also be translated breath. Therefore we would be perfectly in keeping with the Greek language to refer to him as the Holy Breath. We are utterly, totally dependent upon him for life in the Spirit. Without him there is no life. With these facts meeting ready agreement, we ask, "Why are we impotent when we ought to be powerful? Why do our churches struggle along hitting on four cylinders when they ought to be hitting on eight? Why do we live our lives devoid of Christian joy when we could have that effervescence, that exuberance which is the accompaniment of a life lived for Jesus Christ?"

There are several reasons that could be given in answer to these questions. Perhaps the first and the most important is our ignorance of who the Holy Spirit is and what he is capable of doing. We don't give enough time in our study of him. We don't search God's Word to discover how the Holy Spirit has acted in other times and in other experiences. We refer to him almost not at all in the lessons and devotionals we present.

I remember an incident from my early ministry which made an indelible impression upon my mind. It was in my first pastorate out of the seminary. There was a family in that church whom I considered my good friends. I had had the privilege of baptizing the husband, the wife, and two of the children. One day a Sunday School teacher said, "Preacher, did you know that this lady had joined a "holiness church?" I looked at her in amazement and replied, "No, I did not know." After some conversation I suggested she let me visit in that home and find out what happened. I went that very day and was invited in, receiving the same hospitality I had always met. As we sat in the living room and talked, without any bitterness or heat, just with an effort to know why, I asked what had happened. In all candor the lady replied, "I was asked to attend a revival meeting in that church." I asked, "What happened?" She stated, "In that revival service the preacher told us something I had never heard in a Baptist Church." I hastened to question, "What was it?" Her answer was, "He said I could have the power of the Holy Spirit in my life." "That very night," she continued, "I went into my room and closed the door and on my knees opened my heart to God in totality." She continued, "I was infused with a new power, a new spirit, such as I had never known before. I received the power of the Holy Spirit." I couldn't get away from that indictment of my ministry, for she had sat under my preaching for months and apparently I had never clearly stated the fact that she could be Spirit empowered.

Now hear me! If you've never heard it before, the fact is you can be Spirit-filled and Spirit-empowered.

The one requisite is that you meet God's conditions, which involve total submission to him. When you reach the point of willingness and make the surrender, God's Spirit will do the rest. It may be that we are ignorant of that fact. Let me tell you, if you are living your life in a purposeless way, if you have found little or no meaning for your existance, if there is no joy in your Christian experience, my friend you can be Spirit-led. There is no need for you to continue life like that, for there can come a joy, a peace, a happiness that will be contagious, not only infecting your entire being but also those with whom you come in contact.

Why are our churches impotent when we ought to be powerful dynamos? Maybe it's ignorance or maybe it's our twisting of the doctrine of the Holy Spirit. There are a number of modern-day perversions, in my judgment. Some denominations claim a monopoly on the Holy Spirit. When we observe the antics through which they go, some of us are prone to conclude if they've got the Holy Spirit we don't want him.

I remember when pastor of a country church being invited one night to go to a revival meeting even farther out in the country! My church was five miles out of Magnolia, Mississippi. When you get five miles out of Magnolia, you're in the country. This one was even deeper in the woods, for it was across the state line in Louisiana. It was a one-room church, deep in those piney woods. When we drove up on that dirt road, there were cars parked among the trees all around the little building. When we finally found a place to park and walked up to the building, we found it was filled to overflowing. People were standing on the outside looking in the windows. There were no fans, no means of ventilation other than the Lord's own through open windows. As I began to observe, I heard the woman preacher exhorting the congregation. Some crippled people were brought to the pulpit and some members of the congregation began striking those crippled people with their fists. Someone told me they were trying to help them get the Holy Ghost. As I stood there in my rejection of this scene, I determined if that's the way to get the Holy Spirit, I don't want him. My immediate reaction to this kind of attack would be retaliation. I expect yours would be, too. I find no precedent in the New Testament for anything of that nature. I rather find the one requisite for the empowerment of God's Spirit is submission to God's will.

Because of the activities of some denominations we have said, if they have got the Holy Spirit, and if that is what happens when you get him, we don't want him. Yet if we are without him we are without hope and without strength. Maybe we are impotent today because of a misunderstanding of who he is.

There are some errors in the translation of the King James version of the New Testament. Some of these are found in the eighth chapter of Romans in referring to the Holy Spirit. The Holy Spirit is referred to in the neuter gender rather than in the masculine. This is in error, for the Holy Spirit in the original language is always referred to with a masculine pronoun. These mistakes in the eighth chapter of Romans in King James reveal, "the Spirit *itself* beareth witness with our spirit." I believe there are two places in this chapter where the neuter pronoun is used. On the basis of that maybe some of us have concluded that the Holy Spirit is an atmosphere or an innate desire, or an aura in which we live our lives. Nothing could be farther from the truth. The Holy Spirit is a living personality. He is the living Christ living in us. When we come to understand that, when we grasp the truth that the Christian faith is a personal relationship with Christ, when we know that Christ in us empowers us to do his will, then we are in a position to be little Christs in the world in which we live, in the places of responsibility that we hold.

Maybe another reason our churches are impotent is because of our ability to rationalize. Most of us are rather adept at rationalizing our shortcomings. Many of us have come to equate activity with the power and work of the Holy Spirit. The more active a person is, the more likely we are to believe that he is Spirit-directed and Spirit-empowered. That may be true. It may well be that those who are most active are most Spirit-filled, but not necessarily. I can think of exceptions to this. I remember one time a frantic lady called the church office. She asked for me, and when I answered it took a few moments to calm her down to determine why she had called. Finally she got hold of herself enough to blurt out, "Preacher, if you don't give me something to do at the church, I'm going to lose my mind." It just happened that I knew something of the background that caused her to call and make that statement!

She and her husband were the parents of an only child, a daughter. She was a fine young lady. She had grown up and finished high school and had gone away to attend a university. In her freshman year, having been gone from home from September to December, longer at one time than ever before in her life, her parents missed her very much. You can imagine their anticipation of the Christmas holidays. When she came home Christmas, she opened the door into the living room with her parents sitting waiting for her with bated breath. When they rushed up to put their arms around their only daughter and tell her how much they had missed her and how much they loved her, she stepped back with a big smile and said, "Mother and Dad, I want you to meet your new son-in-law." She had married one of those big, burly football players. She hadn't bothered to forewarn them, so you can imagine their consternation. They toughed it out, made the best of it over the holidays, but when the daughter and son-in-law returned, the mother went to pieces. She said, "If you don't give me a job down at the church, I'm going to lose my mind." Now is that necessarily the prompting of God's Spirit? No, not necessarily! You see, it is possible to be active in the work of a local church for selfish purposes. Every movement of the grass is not necessarily the Holy Spirit. It may be a snake in the grass. Every blowing of the wind does not signify the moving of God's Spirit.

It is possible for us to rationalize to the point that we believe the more active we are, the more jobs we have, the more titles we hold, the more Spirit-empowered we are. This is not necessarily so, for God's Word also admonishes us, "Be still and know that I am God."

Let me point out three ways in which we must know the Holy Spirit. There can be no deviation from this, for these are grounded in the truths of God's Word. First, we must know the Holy Spirit in the

Conviction

of sin. The fact is, we are not saved unless or until we have been convicted of sin. Jesus Christ came into the world to seek and to save that which is lost. This means that those who are not lost need no salvation. If you've never sinned you have no need of a Savior. Even when you have sinned, you don't become aware of the penalty and condemnation of sin until God's Spirit impresses your heart with that fact. You can't convict yourself of sin. You can be sorry you have been caught. You can regret the fact that others discovered your transgression, but you can never be convicted for sin until the Holy Spirit does the convicting.

There is no other way of salvation. This is not Baptists' way of being saved. This is God's way. Jesus said the task of the Holy Spirit is to "convict the world of sin." That's not our job, it's his.

It is our job to point out sin, it is our responsibility to avoid it, but it is not our responsibility to convict other people. That's his job. He does it sometimes in mysterious ways. There aren't two ways of salvation. There is only one. That one way is for a sinner to be convicted by the power of God's Spirit and in his conviction cry out for help to Jesus Christ. If we know the Holy Spirit aright, we must know him in conviction and we must know him as a

Companion

Every reference in the New Testament to the Holy Spirit refers to him as a person. He loves, he has intelligence, he can be grieved, he makes intercession for us with groanings. He is a living personality. He comes to live in us, convicting us of the error of our ways and pointing us to paths of righteousness.

When he lives in us, when he comes into our hearts and abides, there is an immediate difference in administration. We are no longer the administrators of our lives, we simply respond to his administration. We no longer pick and choose our own way, we allow him to point us in the direction we should take. This is all part and parcel of making Christ Lord. If Jesus is the Lord of our lives, if he who is the King of the kingdom of God is Lord of all, that means anything he says, we do. Any command he issues, we follow. Any order he gives, we respond to immediately and without question. This is what it means for the Holy Spirit to live in us as our Companion.

There is not only a difference in administration, there comes to be a difference in aspiration. The things that we aspire to change when the Spirit of God lives in us. This is the area of concern of the young people in our day, and I'm grateful for it. They have pointed out the hypocrisy of our continued materialism, all the while claiming Christ as Lord of our lives. If Christ is the Lord of our lives, we shall not be consumed by materialistic concerns! These have a place, for we can't live without food or clothing. But Jesus said, "Take no thought," or don't be anxious for your life, what ye shall eat and what ye shall drink or what ye shall put on, for the Lord who clothes the grass of the field and adorns the lilies of the fields, that same One knows what you need before you need it.

I often wonder at the dichotomy in standards that exist for Christians. We have one set of standards for laymen and another set of standards for preachers. Sometimes we make fun of preachers and laugh at them. We say, "Yeah, he just moved for more money." Now friend is that wrong? Be careful what you say, for if it's wrong for a preacher to move for more money, it's just as wrong for you.

What about these folks that take a transfer from their company from here to Colorado where they can ski in the wintertime? Is that wrong? If it's wrong for a preacher, it's wrong for a layman. You see, God doesn't have two standards. He doesn't have one standard for a preacher and another standard for businessmen. He has the same standard for everyone.

When the Holy Spirit lives within us as our companion, there's a difference in aspiration. There's a difference in whom we are trying to please, what we are seeking to accomplish, and those things with which we occupy our time day after day. That's the difference the Holy Spirit makes.

"Ye shall receive power after the Holy Ghost is come upon you." That's first. Maybe the reason we are not witnesses in our Jerusalem or our Judea or Samaria is that we have not yet let the power of God's Holy Ghost come upon us.

One final word. If we're rightly related to God and the Holy Spirit we must know him as

Continuous

By that I mean he is not a fair-weather friend. He is not one who gives joy during adolescent years and then allows joy to turn to ashes during young manhood or womanhood and through old age. Not at all. He is One who never leaves nor forsakes us.

What's the problem with those who have dropped out in the work of the Kingdom? Maybe they misunderstood the continuity of the presence of the Holy Spirit. He's the one of whom Jesus was speaking when he said, "I'll never leave you nor forsake you." He's the one of whom Jesus was speaking when he said, "Lo, I am with you alway, even into the age of the age," into that period beyond the human mind's power to grasp. Into the age of the age, I'll be with you. Never leave you. Never forsake you.

I've talked to adults in our city, mature men up in years who have said, "Landrum, I don't want to join the church until I'm sure I can hold out. I don't want to be a hypocrite about it and I want to know for sure that I'll be able to hold out when I come." That sounds sincere. On the face of it we would all agree. No one wants a hypocrite to come into the church. On the other hand, if we were to apply that same standard to every area of life, we'd never get married would we? Do you know when you marry that it's going to last? No, all you know is that you're going to give yourself to the marriage, that you're going to invest every vestige of your being into making a successful marriage relationship. When you do that, that's all you can do.

If you come into the kingdom of God aware of your weakness, knowing your inability to hold out by yourself, but knowing that in his power and his strength you will be kept forever, then you are in a position to serve Christ. He is not a fair-weather friend—with you only when the sun is shining—but One who will be with you in the dark days of life as well as the bright. He is One who will stand by your side in weakness as well as strength, who'll not depart from you in sickness or in health. When you understand this about him, you can face life with courage and hope. The Holy Spirit and you! "You shall receive power when the Holy Spirit comes upon you." and then you'll be a witness everywhere you go, at home and abroad. To know him aright, you must know him in conviction, as a companion, and you must know him as continuous, unending in his presence and in his power!

9

WHY WORRY?

The King James translation of verse 31 of the sixth chapter of Matthew leaves a great deal to be desired. The translation reads, "Take no thought for tomorrow." This is the translation of a Greek noun which basically means "to be drawn in different directions." I think Phillips has the better rendering of this word as he translates it into English with the one word, "worry." "Don't be worried about tomorrow." There's a good reason for Jesus to have said this and we will see in this text why he said there was no reason to worry.

It has been suggested that this word is a combination of two others which describe "a divided mind."

You get here a very clear picture of this sin that we call worry. What is worry? Worry is a divided mind, a mind that is torn between two things, consequently it is unable to concentrate on one thing. This is the manner is which many people are dissipating their personalities. We seem to be caught on the horns of the dilemma between worthwhile interests and nonessential things. When worry grips us we have a difficult time deciding between important matters and unimportant interests. The result ordinarily is that we accomplish little or nothing in life.

In Matthew 6:22 Jesus said, "If therefore thine eye be single, thy whole body shall be full of light." In this context the eye merely becomes the window of the mind. The way to have an undivided mind, a mind free of worry, is to have a single eye—an eye fixed upon one purpose and which never removes its gaze or its intent stare from that purpose. If your eye is single your whole body will be filled with light, and "light" means something altogether good and wonderful. If you want joy in life, if you want the abundance that Jesus Christ offers, it will come when your eye is single, when your mind is not divided.

The apostle James said, "A double-minded man is unstable in all his ways." He is giving support to this same teaching from the lips of Jesus. A double-minded man, a man who is trying to do two things simultaneously, who is trying to give first loyalty to more than one cause, is a man who is unstable and cannot be counted on by either cause.

Did you know it's an impossibility to be a citizen of two nations simultaneously? You cannot be an American citizen and at the same time be a citizen of any other nation in the world. Citizenship in one rules out citizenship in the other. By that same token, in the spiritual realm, when we become citizens of the kingdom of God we are no longer citizens of the kingdom of Satan. The devil, Satan, is the prince of the powers of this world, and when we have given first allegiance to Jesus Christ this rules out the allegiance to Satan. The problem that most of us have in Christian living is our inability to decide in which Kingdom we wish to live. We want to be citizens of both and this presents conflict. This is where worry comes in, and it often has serious mental and physical implications.

A Negro preacher friend gave me a rich insight when he said, "No, it's not hard to be a Christian." I thought for a moment and I wanted to hear what he said from there. He said, "It's easy to be a Christian. What's hard is trying to be a Christian when you're living like the devil." That's the problem, isn't it? That's what gets to be hard, when we're caught on the horns of the dilemma between things that are right and of first magnitude and things that actually mean little or nothing. This is what makes us double-minded and unstable. Who is the worried person? The worried person is the one who has double vision, the one whose eye is not single. He cannot focus upon one thing. Our subject is worry, and we're dealing with it from the Christian perspective. Let me clarify the

Problem

in the first place. Many medical doctors say that numbers of their patients state as their first complaint, "I can't sleep at night." Ask your medical doctor about the frequency of this complaint. "I can't sleep at night." Why can't people sleep at night? Worry is the prime reason! Peace of mind that enables one to sleep and derive rest for his physical body comes from an undivided mind. Paul did not suffer from the sin of worry, for his mind was single. He said, "This one thing I do."

Think of what worry does. It affects the emotions and when it divides the emotions it leaves us in a state of flux and change and instability. A worried person is marked by emotional extremes, either being exuberant in happiness or depressed in gloom. He can never get any true enjoyment out of life. He's always concerned about something that might happen or some possibility. Worry divides our emotions.

Worry divides our understanding and the result is uncertainty and to be left with no clear-cut convictions. Worry keeps us from grasping things. We've had a great emphasis in our day on the open mind. It's a little bit of a status symbol to be said to be open-minded, and I'm for that. There are things about which all of us should keep open minds. I have an open mind concerning life in the universe and on some of the planets. All of the evidence is not in, and my mind is open at that point. But there are some things on which my open mind has closed, once and for all. I have absolutely no doubt concerning the deity, the divinity of Jesus Christ. I have no doubt and no reservation concerning the credibility of the Book. I have no doubt about the virgin birth of our Lord and about his imminent return. My open mind has closed on some things and it occurs to me that this is the purpose of an open mind. Keep it open until you find truth and then close it upon those facts. Worry causes our understanding to be divided and when our understanding is divided we don't really believe anything. We don't have any deep, clear-cut convictions.

Worry divides our sense of purpose and results in failure to finish what we start. How many tasks can you look to and say, "This is a completed job. This is a responsibility that fell to me, I accepted it and finished it." If you are a worried person, there are not many completed tasks to which you can point. Worry divides our sense of purpose and we never seem to get anything done. Just like the children of Israel in the wilderness, we go around and around in circles for forty years. I know people like that and so do you, but the question is "Am I like that?" Are you like that? Are you a worrier?

You know, worry preoccupies and when on occasion we are suddenly jerked to reality, we are face to face with some decisions that have to be made and we make those decisions on the spur of the moment. Most of the time those are the wrong decisions. It stems from worry which has preoccupied. We've been concerned with so many other things we haven't been able to concentrate on making a clear-cut, intelligent decision on the one thing that really matters.

Worry is the cause of many marital difficulties. As I sit in my office from day to day, person after person comes with a problem. Most of these problems have to do with marriage and the home. Worry about the home is a state of a divided mind. Maybe the divided mind in the home is because of a third party. Maybe there's another man, or another woman. It may be the mind is divided over business matters and money problems and those worries keep a house from ever becoming a home for those who live in it.

It can well be that the home is on the rocks because the wife has a divided mind and simply can't make up her mind between her husband and "mama." She constantly is caught on the horns of this dilemma and that worry, that divided mind, keeps a home from being a little oasis of bliss and happiness. Maybe the divided mind is due to an egocentric and a hellish preoccupation with the children and the home, to which the wife gives her undivided loyalty, while defaulting in her God-given responsibilities to her husband. Many a home has gone on the rocks because of that.

Possibly the worry is due to a total commitment on the part of a husband and father to business or to making a living. He develops the feeling, egotistically, that after all he is responsible for putting bread on the table. Why shouldn't someone else take over all the other obligations? This is a divided mind. It's divided over two loyalties and there will never be any happiness for one who makes the wrong choice in this area, for when one gives his total allegiance to business and making a living, he forgets his obligations and responsibilities as a husband and father and head of the house. This is just touching the hem of the garment of the problems that stem from worry or a divided mind. But I want to focus on two other factors before we get to the positive note. These two factors are

Pity and Procrastination

I think it has well been said that there are two days in every week about which we should never be worried. Start from this point if you're a worrier. There are two days in every week about which you need have no fear or worries. Those two days are yesterday and tomorrow! Those are two days in which you cannot live, two days that should be kept entirely free and clean of all worries. You can't live yesterday. You can't live tomorrow. You must live for today.

In the main those who live yesterday over and over and over again are guilty of a sort of self-pity. They indulge themselves in a kind of daydream in which they play the game, "I wish." This may be a teen-ager who in his frustration and rebellion against life as it is says, "Stop the world, I want to get off." The teen-ager making a statement of that kind is asking, "Why was I ever born? What am I even doing here?"

The divided mind marks the man who asks, "Why did I ever take this job?" I've heard men ask that after working at a job for twenty-five years. After a quarter of a century on the same job they are still asking, "Why did I ever take this job?" Maybe he is questioning whether or not he has chosen the right vocation, but whatever it is in the subconscious mind, he is revealing a divided mind. He has no singleness of purpose. He never has accepted his responsibility and said, "This one thing I do." Consequently he has never given his best to that job, even though he may have performed it in a perfunctory manner for twenty-five years.

The question that divides the mind of some women is, "Why did I ever marry him?" Some of you may have asked that. You may have never articulated it, but you've thought about it. Why did I ever marry this one? This reveals a divided mind because she is asking herself what life would have been like if she had married the captain of the basketball team instead of the captain of the football team! She made her choice, but she spends her life wondering what it would have been like if. . . . The divided mind of that wife and mother keeps her from ever giving single minded attention to the establishment and development of her own home and to the making of a successful marriage. There can be no successful marriage when a mind is divided like this. Yesterday is gone. You must begin with that fact. Yesterday is gone, it cannot be relived. It cannot be undone or redone. Yesterday is past forever and forever. No deed may be undone, no word may be erased. The loved one who has died is not coming back. Yesterday is in the past. How foolish we are to sit in self-pity trying to bring back things of yesterday.

The psalmist must have had this in mind when he said, "This is the day that the Lord hath made, let us rejoice and be glad in it." You can thank God that you are alive. Maybe you've lost a loved one, maybe you've had business reverses, maybe your friends have left you, maybe your company has transferred you to a new community, maybe you've got Vietnam staring you in the face. "This is the day that the Lord hath made, let us rejoice and let us be glad in it." Be done with the pity that causes you to live in the yesterdays.

You know, it's equally sinful to try to live in that day called tomorrow. This worrisome sin is sometimes called procrastination. If we try to live yesterday, that's a form of self-pity. If we try to live tomorrow, that's procrastination and neither one of these is extolled and exonerated in the Word of God. It has been well said that yesterday is gone, tomorrow never comes. You may promise your tomorrow to God, but hear me friend, God has never promised a tomorrow to you. There are people right now promising God their to-morrows. You'd better underscore the fact that God never promised you one. You are making foolish prom-ises when you promise God something that you don't have. Thousands of people are living in their tomor-rows. They're guilty of the sin of procrastination that causes a divided mind and results in worry, the dissipa-tion of one's physical energies, and the accomplishment of nothing!

I know people who are saying, "Tomorrow I'm going to quit smoking." I know others who have said, "To-morrow I'm going to quit drinking. I'm going to put it aside, walk away and leave it." I know others who have said, "Tomorrow I'm going on a diet." There are still others who have said, "Tomorrow I am going to start tithing. Just as soon as I get all my business affairs straightened out, then I'm going to be honest with God." Still others have said, "Tomorrow I'm going to start saving some money and quit spending everything I make. I'm going to start setting a little aside for a possible rainy day." Then many, many people have said, "Tomorrow, I'm going to take my stand for Jesus. I'm going to walk down the aisle of the church and say, I'm trusting Jesus as my Savior and I want to be baptized and received into the fellowship of this church." Tomorrow, tomorrow, tomorrow. In your mind there is a division. It is a division between what you're doing now that you ought not to be doing and the tomorrow, which may never come, in which you've already decided you're going to do better.

The problem of worry is focused in these two categories, yesterday and tomorrow, pity and procrastination. We know what we ought to do but we simply do not do it. Myriads of people have made a spectre out of tomorrow by worry, anxiety, and fear. You keep putting off until tomorrow things that you hope will go away and you never face up to them, never encounter them head-on and never make a decision. You keep delaying and worry about it and worry results in an ulcer or things just as physically debilitating. Tomorrow never comes. Yesterday is gone forever. Procrastination is the thief of time. Fear and worry over tomorrow will keep us from living today. Now how can we cope with this problem? If you've got your finger on the text,

we're going to find God's
        Provision
here in the sixth chapter of Matthew. In verse 25 Jesus
told us why we need not worry. What did he say? God
has given us life and since life is the highest and best
gift that God gives, we can trust God to sustain it. You
don't have to worry about life, God gave it to you, and
God will preserve it as long as it is in his purpose. In
verse 26 he said: Take a look at the birds. They don't
worry about food and God feeds them, so why should
you worry? You are a higher creation of almighty God
than a bird. God doesn't look upon a bird in the same
way that he looks on you. Birds aren't made in the
image of God, man is. If God feeds those little birds and
they're a lesser creation, what are you worried about?
God will feed you also.

In verse 27 Jesus asked, "Why worry?" He points out
that "a short man can't become taller by worrying." I
don't know, but Jesus could have been looking at a
fellow the size of Zaccheus. Zaccheus could have spent
his days worrying because he was a short man instead
of a tall man, but Jesus said, "A short man can't 'worry
on' additional inches." This is not something to be worried about. God gave you life, he gave you your body.
Just take what he has given you and begin to use it.
Don't worry about things that might have been or
could have been or should have been. Consider what
you can do right now and then don't worry, because
you can do it. In verse 30 Jesus said, "It's a lack of faith

that causes you to worry."

In verse 28 he said, "It's ridiculous for you to worry about what you're going to wear." How many men have heard their wives say before church time, "I haven't got a thing to wear." Have you ever heard that? If you are a husband you have. You don't have to worry about what you're going to put on, for God clothes the flowers in the field. Just wear what you've got, because "man looketh on the outward appearance, but God looketh on the heart." Worry is a lack of faith. That's the way of pagans and the word that appears here, "Gentiles," means the "nations." Obviously it had a reference to those that were outside the faith. This is the way of pagans, the way of worry. Those of us who know the one true God, the God of Abraham, Isaac, and Jacob, who revealed himself in flesh in Jesus Christ, the God of love and mercy, know he'll take care of us if we are trying to serve him.

Then Jesus gave us two positive values that are just as viable today as they were then. First, if you really do know God in Jesus Christ, then seek first his Kingdom and watch how he'll take care of all these other things. If you really do know him, put his Kingdom first. When you establish that priority, the God who feeds the sparrows, the God who clothes the lilies of the field, the God who has given you life will sustain it and take care of your actual needs. This is a guaranteed prescription spoken by the voice of almighty God through Jesus Christ.

There's a second part to the prescription. It is spoken in the omniscience and power of heaven. In verse 34, Jesus Christ, the world's greatest psychiatrist, gave advice which psychiatrists are giving in this very hour. That advice is, "Live only one day at a time." That's the premise upon which A.A. builds its ministry and enlists its members: live one day at a time. This is the advice given to people on the couches of psychiatrists from one end of this world to the other—live one day at a time. If you spend your time on earth living each day to the fullest, give single-minded devotion to things that matter. Do every task the best you are capable of doing it, and then you haven't anything to worry about. Determine what God wants you to do and then do it, and do it with the totality of your being. Do it for the glory of God, and when you lie down at night you will have nothing to worry about. There is no divided mind if you have put yourself to a task, brought it to completion and have left the results in the hand of God.

You know, you can begin this sort of process by living for this very moment. You can make this moment in life meaningful if you commit your life in faith to Jesus for salvation, or if you commit your life, your talents, your all to Jesus for service through his church.